Facing It Out

Tavistock Clinic Series
Nick Temple, Margot Waddell (Series Editors)
Published and distributed by Karnac Books

Other titles in the Tavistock Clinic Series:

Assessment in Child Psychotherapy
Margaret Rustin and Emanuela Quagliata (editors)

Inside Lives: Psychoanalysis and the Growth of the Personality
Margot Waddell

Internal Landscapes and Foreign Bodies:
Eating Disorders and Other Pathologies
Gianna Williams

Mirror to Nature: Drama, Psychoanalysis and Society
Margaret Rustin and Michael Rustin

Multiple Voices: Narrative in Systemic Family Psychotherapy
Renos K. Papadopoulos and John Byng-Hall (editors)

Psychoanalysis and Culture: A Kleinian Perspective
David Bell (editor)

Psychotic States in Children
Margaret Rustin, Maria Rhode, Alex Dubinsky,
Hélène Dubinsky (editors)

Reason and Passion: A Celebration of the Work of Hanna Segal
David Bell (editor)

Sent Before My Time: A Child Psychotherapist's View of Life on a
Neonatal Intensive Care Unit
Margaret Cohen

Surviving Space: Papers on Infant Observation
Andrew Briggs (editor)

Therapeutic Care for Refugees: No Place Like Home
Renos K. Papadopoulos (editor)

Understanding Trauma: A Psychoanalytic Approach
Caroline Garland (editor)

Orders: Tel: +44 (0)20 8969 4454; Fax: +44 (0)20 8969 5585
         Email: shop@karnacbooks.com; Internet: www.karnacbooks.com

Facing It Out

Clinical Perspectives on Adolescent Disturbance

edited by
Robin Anderson
Anna Dartington

KARNAC
LONDON   NEW YORK

First published in 1998 by Gerald Duckworth & Co. Ltd.
Second impression 1999
This edition printed in 2002 by
H. Karnac (Books) Ltd
118 Finchley Road, London, NW3 5HT
www.karnacbooks.com

Reprinted 2003, 2004, 2007

A catalogue record for this book is available
from the British Library

ISBN 978-1-85575-967-1

Edition amendments by The Studio Publishing Services Ltd, Exeter, EX4 8JN
Printed by the MPG Books Group in the UK

Contents

Contents

Series Editors' Preface

Since it was founded in 1920, the Tavistock Clinic has developed a wide range of therapeutic approaches to mental health which have been strongly influenced by the ideas of psychoanalysis. It has also adopted systemic family therapy as a theoretical model and a clinical approach to family problems. The Clinic is now the largest training institution in Britain for mental health, providing postgraduate and qualifying courses in social work, psychology, psychiatry, and child, adolescent, and adult psychotherapy, as well as in nursing and primary care. It trains about 1,400 students each year in over 45 courses.

The Clinic's philosophy aims at promoting therapeutic methods in mental health. Its work is founded on the clinical expertise that is also the basis of its consultancy and research activities. The aim of this Series is to make available to the reading public the clinical, theoretical, and research work that is most influential at the Tavistock Clinic. The Series sets out new approaches in the understanding and treatment of psychological disturbance in children, adolescents, and adults, both as individuals and in families.

This book is based on the wealth of experience gathered in the forty years of the life of the Adolescent Department at the Clinic. It covers a full range of clinical work with some of the most difficult areas of adolescence, but it also gives a conceptual framework of normal adolescence and traces the difficulties that arise when this goes wrong. *Facing It Out* presents new work which has not previously been fully described. The book will be vital reading for clinicians whose practice includes work with adolescents, and will also be of fundamental value to others studying the processes of adolescence, such as parents, teachers, social workers and probation officers.

Nicholas Temple and Margot Waddell
Series Editors

Acknowledgements

The editors would like to express their particular thanks to Jocelyne Phiniefs and Sandra Masterson for their patience, support and administrative expertise. We are also grateful to the Adolescent Department collectively for their interest and encouragement in our endeavours.

Our thanks to Faber and Faber for permission to reproduce excerpts from the poems 'Lady Lazarus' and 'Daddy' from the Sylvia Plath collection, also to the Institute of Psycho-Analysis for permission to publish a revised version of Gianna Williams' paper 'Reflections of Some Dynamics of Eating Disorders: No Entry Defences and Foreign Bodies', first published in the *International Journal of Psychoanalysis* 1997, Part 4 Vol. 78.

Finally but foremost our thanks to our patients who put their trust in us.

Robin Anderson
Anna Dartington

Foreword

'Facing it out' is a challenge and a history. It sounds determined and 'Churchillean' in tone in that it inspires enthusiasm and effort which will be revealed as the book is read.

Many times during my work in a forward area in the Burma Campaign in the early 1940s, doing what was called Forward Psychiatry, I met senior colleagues who told me about the Tavistock Clinic. I was interested in the psychodynamic approach and by then had realised already the fact that an emotional breakdown was made more chronic for every 100 miles the psychiatric casualty needed to be evacuated away from the battle area and the comrades he knew and liked. I was impressed that the Tavistock medical staff seemed to know how to deal with the complicated therapeutic task with which we were confronted. They seemed to be interested in understanding and solving these problems both from a scientific and human perspective.

After the war was over it was many years before I managed to obtain a post at the Tavistock Clinic, and was then a 'foiled circuitous wanderer'. This was in 1962. In 1966 the large modern building was built and consequently projects and work with patients were greatly facilitated. Thus it was possible for the Adolescent Department to have a proper home of its own.

In 1969 my work in the Tavistock Clinic was increased and I was based in the Adolescent Department. From then until I retired in 1979 was the happiest professional time in my life. 'How can we do it' was the question, not 'How can we avoid doing it'. In the three departments and the closely associated Tavistock Institute of Human Relations, there was a constant flux of creative enthusiasm dynamised by a devotion to both intrapsychic work and work on the complexities of interpersonal relationships. This attention both to the external struggles in the world of adolescents and the significance of their deepest inner feelings is what is special about the Tavistock Clinic and the work of the Adolescent

Department. I have encountered nothing like it anywhere else in the world.

The battlefields may look very different, but the environment of our 1990s inner cities does not provide an easy setting for development and the young people who succumb are no less in need of help. Often what is lost is the capacity to have hope. Without it whatever resources there may be available cannot be utilised. One of the primary therapeutic tasks in working with young people and their parents is to help them recover hope but this requires those working with them to have the inner and collective resources to sustain themselves against all-pervading despair which can so easily infect those who work with the mentally ill.

I am very glad that the current generation of clinicians in the Adolescent Department is continuing to provide this unique combination of science and humanity to the current generation of adolescent casualties.

A. Hyatt Williams

Contributors

Robin Anderson, Consultant Psychiatrist and Psychoanalyst, Adolescent Department, Tavistock Clinic.

Jonathan Bradley, Consultant Child and Adolescent Psychotherapist, Adolescent Department, Tavistock Clinic. Head of Child Psychotherapy Services, City and Hackney NHS Community Trust.

Stephen Briggs, Senior Clinical Lecturer in Social Work, Adolescent Department, Tavistock Clinic. Senior Lecturer in the Department of Human Relations at the University of East London.

Anna Dartington, Senior Clinical Lecturer in Social Work and Psychoanalytic Psychotherapist, Adolescent Department, Tavistock Clinic.

Hélène Dubinsky, Consultant Child and Adolescent Psychotherapist, Adolescent Department, Tavistock Clinic.

Richard Graham, Consultant Child and Adolescent Psychiatrist, Watford and Borehamwood Child and Family Clinics.

Lynda Miller, Consultant Child and Adolescent Psychotherapist, Joint Head of the Learning Disability Service, Tavistock Clinic. Principal Child and Adolescent Psychotherapist, Enfield Child Guidance Clinic.

Elizabeth Oliver-Bellasis, Senior Clinical Lecturer in Social Work, Child and Adolescent Psychotherapist, formerly Chair, Young People's Counselling Service, Adolescent Department, Tavistock Clinic.

Paul Upson, Consultant Clinical Psychologist, Psychoanalytic Psychotherapist, Adolescent Department, Tavistock Clinic.

Contributors

Margot Waddell, Consultant Child and Adolescent Psychotherapist and Psychoanalyst, Adolescent Department, Tavistock Clinic.

Gianna Williams, Consultant Child and Adolescent Psychotherapist, Adolescent Department, Tavistock Clinic.

Introduction

Robin Anderson and Anna Dartington

The idea to develop a department for adolescents in the Tavistock Clinic was formed in the mind of Dr Derek Miller, a young English psychiatrist who had been working during the 1950s at the Menninger Clinic in the USA. As we know the 1950s was a time when adolescents and young people, soon to be classified as 'teenagers', were becoming increasingly popular as a subject of both celebration and investigation in the public mind. This was happening not only in America but also throughout Europe, and the upsurge of interest in young people characterised by an intense curiosity was clearly reflected by the media in all its forms.

In 1951 J.D. Salinger had written *Catcher in the Rye*, one of the first post-war novels that seemed to proclaim the age of the teenager who demanded to have an independent and autonomous voice. Salinger's teenage character, Holden Caulfield is likeable, he is not a brat, he even has a willingness to please. It's just that he cannot see a way into adult life that won't turn him into one of the 'phoneys' he instinctively suspects. Caulfield's keenly critical observation of the adult world seemed to herald the phenomenon of teenager as sceptic. Many 'teenage' films were to follow, for example, *The Wild One* in 1954 which starred Marlon Brando, and in 1955 *Rebel Without a Cause* which featured a new actor named James Dean. Both of these films emanated a heady mixture of overt sexuality and casual violence. Understandably, young people started to find themselves extremely interesting.

The idea of adolescence as a prolonged transitional phase seems to be very much a twentieth century phenomenon and it is interesting to speculate about the influences which brought about this particular advent of 'adolescence' during the 1950s. A popular and highly credible explanation is that, following another round of horrific slaughter of young men in particular in a World War, society was in a state of manic reparation needing to appease youth and to idealise the new generation.

1

It is possible, for example, that the enormous publicity surrounding Elvis Presley's entry into the Army is some sort of validation for this interpretation of events. It will be remembered that Presley was all smiles as he was filmed receiving his regulation Army haircut and despite the publicity everybody knew that the institutional representatives of the parental generation were not going to allow this particular young man to die in combat.

By the time that Derek Miller was crossing the Atlantic on his way back to London in 1959 to set up the Adolescent Department in the Tavistock Clinic, there was already an eager market of young people who wished to discuss their preoccupations, interests and problems with adult professionals who were outside the daily intimacies and expectations of the family network.

Adolescence is one of the most radical of all the developmental periods. In the few years between the onset of puberty and adulthood, one's sense of oneself must adapt to the physical changes of size, shape, strength, of changes in build, changes in appearance, changes in the sound of the voice, being sexually mature; for boys being able to impregnate and an exponential increase in strength, and for girls to carry a pregnancy, to have breasts and to have periods. The social and psychic corollaries of this are to develop the capacity to become intimate with others, to form sexual relationships, to become less dependent on parents, and to move towards separation from the family. To survive that modern initiation of manhood and womanhood, GCSEs and A levels and the securing of a job. In short, to move towards becoming an independent person, both internally and externally.

The list is incomplete but it is meant to convey that there is no sphere of life that is untouched by changes at this time – not only is the world never the same again but you are never the same again. Yet at the heart of the infant self and its early object relationships there is a core of unchangeability. And here lies a tremendous source of tension; that part of us wants never to have to give up our early desires and the means of gratifying them and now is confronted by changes that more than ever are in conflict with this world. Sometimes directly opposing old satisfactions and at others, threatening the self because it offers the infant self the power to gratify some of its most dangerous wishes – both sexual and violent ones.

Kafka's short novel, *Metamorphosis*, about a young man who wakes up one day to find that he has become an insect, captures a more paranoid nightmare version of what happens when a new kind of body has to be encountered and lived in. It is extraordinary to think that a

2

12-year-old is just about, and usually with a terrible cost, able to move into a precocious and precarious independent existence. Long before adolescence was invented Lord Nelson was described, shaking his head and muttering, 'Too young, too young' as he saw the 11-year-old little boys who were Midshipmen in the 18th century Royal Navy. And yet at this same time, there had recently been a Prime Minister of England taking office at 24 – William Pitt in 1783. Such a metamorphosis requires enormous psychic work.

By the time children arrive at puberty, most of them have by some means or other achieved some kind of balance, but this balance depends on the world being relatively stable both internally and externally. Puberty and what follows are quite the opposite. The work of adolescence can be compared with Freud's description of the work of mourning in 'Mourning and Melancholia' (1915). The ego is required to examine every aspect of the lost object – the lost relationship – to pick up each particular aspect of the relationship, explore it, remember it and face the loss in order to let it go. If the adolescent is to successfully achieve adulthood, he must re-negotiate every aspect of his relationship with himself and with his external and internal objects in a new context – this activity is what we often refer to as *the adolescent process*. It is like a review of the life that has been lived so far. In contrast to the latency child, all adolescents have to deal with this changing world and the experience of being out of balance to some extent. Indeed, it seems to be those young people who have the inner strength and resources to bear to continue the experience of being naturally out of balance, as well as an environment that can support this, who can achieve the best adjustment in adult life. A colleague whose adolescence was spent as a refugee from Nazi persecution in the last war reported that it was not safe enough then to have an adolescence. The kinds of experiments in new relationships or new ways of relating just felt too dangerous.

The whole psychic climate during adolescence moves slowly in the direction of a change in the degree to which one needs to face reality. Before puberty, much of psychic development could remain in a certain sense provisional; certain desires for oneself or one's objects need not be actively renounced. But in this new situation, the consequences of not facing certain 'facts of life', are much more serious.

It is this beginning sense that what we do in adolescence is closer to the realities of adult life that increases the young person's need to cope with anxiety – the price of not managing is greater. Even at its most simple, young adolescents usually begin to show more independence from their parents, but if they are more in charge of their lives and who they spend parts of it with, then the price of their not managing is much greater, indeed at the most extreme, death, if they cannot avoid putting themselves in danger.

We have referred to the complex relationship young people and the adult world have with each other and have offered some thoughts about what adolescence means to us adults, how it provokes our envy as well as our disapproval. But it is also the case that young people are very dependant on adults about whom they often have very divided and contrasting feelings. They require and even compel the adults in their world to react to them often making adults feel they are behaving out of character or that they are at their worst and yet feel helpless to do otherwise so that the task of being a parent during adolescence can be very difficult. Often we can see the problems parents are having not simply as a burden but as a forum for this adult/adolescent interaction, in which important aspects of adolescent development are taking place.

However, this uncomfortable relationship with the adult world is the milieu that professionals working with young people have to work with. The engagement with young people often feels hard won. Frequently young people want to avoid stopping and thinking about themselves. Action is the preferred mode and sitting down with an adult and trying to face up to difficulties often feels for them too much like a retreat to the very dependency they are trying to outgrow. It is particularly difficult for them when they are put in touch with their infant and childhood longings. They can feel as if they have lost their often fragile grip on adulthood and collapsed back into a child world from which they will never escape. For this reason, we attach great importance to how we open a dialogue with our young patients. We try to show them that we respect their fragile sense of separation from their parents often by asking them to contact us themselves even after they have been referred by a parent or a professional. If this is successful, it helps to strengthen their sense of beginning to take responsibility for their lives. We then embark on an assessment phase of a few appointments, during which we are carrying out an assessment in the more usually understood way of looking at their mental state and their disturbance, but also, and vitally for us, of trying to help them to gain a sense of interest in their lives and difficulties, and in this way to help them to find ways in which they can feel they are not simply passive victims of circumstances, but that they may find in themselves the means of tackling their difficulties. This is both the privilege and the burden of adolescence.

It seems that adult generations, either consciously or unconsciously continue to expect the young to represent something for them, it may be hope and idealism, sometimes it is rebellion and sometimes it is even self-sacrifice. In the 1970s a 'punk' generation played with a notion of a nihilistic life. In 1995 a young man in Israel killed the leader of his country, apparently believing it would save his race.

We have selected the chapters to give a sense of the different ways in which adolescents get into difficulties, whether with eating disorders or with depression and a wish to end their lives. Some young people are struggling with adolescence in the context of handicap. Lynda Miller in Chapter 3 describes how she tries to address the very same issues with them in ways that make sense of how they feel about themselves in the world. In Chapter 9, 'The Scapegoat', Margot Waddell looks at a particular phenomenon which, although not unique to adolescence, shows how the wish to disown unwanted parts of the self and to dispose of them gives rise to social consequences especially manifest in the form of racism and of group violence are such serious problems especially amongst some young people.

Paul Upson, in Chapter 11, takes a broad look at a very fundamental problem of establishing a work identity, which is so important and yet so difficult in the modern world where the future is so uncertain with its unemployment, part-time and short-term jobs which require so much more inner security to cope with.

Richard Graham, in Chapter 10, and Anna Dartington in Chapter 1, take a family perspective on adolescence. Anna Dartington explores what it is like for many adolescents who are having to achieve adulthood in the tight circumstances of today's small, often lone parent families. Richard Graham looks at how we try to talk to families and some of the ideas we draw on to help with our conceptualising.

Running through all the chapters in this book is an emphasis on a developmental perspective. Whatever the origins of the young person's difficulties it always interferes in some way with their progress on this pathway so that a central part of our therapeutic aim is to help them deal with whatever has obstructed this journey so that it can be resumed.

We have tried to keep jargon to a minimum as we describe our work but where this is necessary we have tried to explain what we mean in a straightforward way. Of course we are not trying to imply that our work does not require vigorous and lengthy training but we hope in this way to make what we do accessible and of relevance to those who have reason to want to understand young people better.

In this book you will find the adolescents of today, those who are growing up in the late days of the twentieth century, largely unaffected

5

by the stories of the great wars but extremely preoccupied with the violence of their own times. You will meet here those who feel depressed, dislocated or lost. Many will be worried about their parents and resentful about experiences of divorce, migration and re-settlement. Some will feel that they have not been kept in mind and have had to manage painful, even abusive experiences on their own. Others will have experienced loneliness, embarrassment and shame but alongside and above all this there is the young person's capacity to value ordinary common-sense and a humour that can see the world for what it is, so imperfect, so desperately frustrating, but also so potentially full of unexpected pleasure where common understanding and friendship can be found.

1

The Intensity of Adolescence in Small Families

Anna Dartington

This Chapter is about small family groups and how they manage the disturbance of adolescence. I am defining a small family as a group of two or three people who live together, sometimes two parents and a single child but, increasingly commonly, a single parent alone with one or two children. The experience of smallness is intensified when, for various reasons, there is an emotional or geographical distance from a wider family membership.

The thoughts that are gathered here are based on my experience of working with adolescents who are struggling with their parents and parents who are struggling with their adolescents. I will not be discussing family therapy as such in this paper. This is a fascinating subject in its own right and is covered elsewhere in this book (Chapter 10). I will be discussing individuals who seek help alone. This is often because they are feeling seriously misunderstood and hopeless about being heard in the family context. Some present themselves as refugees from an emotional intensity in the family which they find unbearable. Small families are inevitably more vulnerable to intensity because more is expected of a few. When they are also required to accommodate the emotional and behavioural experimentation of adolescence small families may become under considerable pressure.

Perhaps these introductory statements have already suggested something of a paradox. Surely a small family provides an opportunity for everyone to have more attention? This is undoubtedly true. The fact is that most adolescents, particularly in the middle teenage years, do not want to be the focus of attention. At least they do not want attention in the way that adults ordinarily understand it, that is, for example, the attention that entertainers want of their public or lovers want of the beloved or even the attention that small children want from their parents. In the family context most adolescents prefer to be a significant but understated presence, a presence that does not invite comment or scrutiny but at the same time reserves the right to observe and comment on the behaviour of others, most particularly the parents.

This combination of the wish to be inconspicuous and at the same time assuming an attitude of 'knowing best' can be particularly infuriating for parents, particularly if they are themselves unsupported or too stressed to mobilise a sense of proportion, or more to the point, a sense of humour, always the best antidote with which to confront adolescent grandiosity.

What Do Adolescents Really Want From a Family?

I would like to share some of the themes that adolescents and their parents have highlighted when asked what they hope and expect from a family life. The following are examples of some frequently recurring themes.

Protection from Public Shame

Richard aged 15: 'I had a nasty argument with my parents because they found out that I took a chocolate bar from a shop without paying for it. It was a really stupid thing to do. I expect they will keep bringing it up. They may even insist that I go back to apologise to the shopkeeper. At least I can trust them not to tell the neighbours and stuff. If they did I swear I would run away.'

Protection from Unnecessary Humiliation

Mrs B, mother of Ian aged 14: 'We had some new friends round for supper and one of our guests, who is feeling rather beleaguered with two small children at the moment, started to talk about her 4-year-old daughter's bed wetting problem. Unknown to her Ian had experienced the same problem when he was the same age. I saw Ian growing red in the face, obviously desperately worried that somebody would make the connection. I managed to signal to my husband who changed the subject while I found a job for Ian in the kitchen. It all sounds a bit melodramatic in retrospect but I can still remember how painfully self-conscious I felt as a teenager.'

1. The Intensity of Adolescence in Small Families

The Capacity for Negotiation

Mr D, father of Vanessa aged 16 and Janet aged 17: 'Having two girls of this age there is inevitably an enormous issue about staying out late, especially now that the girls are wishing to go to different parties with different friends. My wife and I have had to be very firm at times, despite the odd tantrum that has ensued, nevertheless we do try to remember what it was like at their age.

When I do pick up my daughters from a party we have what we call a 'mutual promise pact' which is that if they promise to be ready to leave at the time we have agreed, that is not to keep me waiting, I will promise to be careful to park around the corner out of the sight of their friends!'

Somewhere to be Private

Julia aged 14: 'My mum read my diary. I know she did because it was moved to a different place. She won't let me clean my own room even though I want to. If she does it again I'm going to ask my father if I can go and live with him.'

Opportunities to Observe How Adults Talk and Relate to Each Other

Helen aged 18: 'I hated it when my parents separated, they said it was mutual but I knew my mother was very upset. She has a new man friend now but he doesn't come to the house because my brother is rude to him.

When I visit my dad's now I quite like it. I like the way that he and his partner laugh together and also the funny things they disagree about. They have a new baby too so now I have a sister which is quite nice. What I like most is the way they include me in things so I can see the way that couples work. I can't remember that with my own parents, probably because I was too young. I really hope that I don't have to go through a divorce.'

The Space to Retreat from Parental Wishes and Desires

Mrs J, mother of Nigel aged 17: 'Nigel and I have always been so close. He was an unexpected baby conceived at the end of an unsatisfactory affair. I can remember the moment when I felt we had begun to separate. When he was 13 he began to smell different, that's when he was starting to become a man.

I have my career and my friends but I dread the time when he leaves for university. My love for him now has to be the love that lets him go. It sounds good in theory but I know it's going to be hard.'

Each of these vignettes present a miniature window into family life, commonplace situations that most of us will recognise. It will be immediately apparent that some of these adolescent concerns, ordinary as they are, have the potential to be more explosive in small families.

Protection from unnecessary shame and humiliation is something that all adolescents need at some time, particularly in their phases of intense self-consciousness. Adolescents can be very difficult to live with in their moods of self-preoccupation and self-doubt, when they are likely to be reclusive at one moment and argumentative at the next. Elder siblings and grandparents can be extremely helpful at such times, providing necessary distractions and helpful mediation in heated family debates. It can be very hard for single parents, particularly if they are distanced from other family members, to be the sole representatives of an adult viewpoint.

Somewhere to be private is a necessity for all family members. In a small family there are more opportunities for this but paradoxically it can be a problem for only children who are often too much the centre of parental attention. This centrality which younger children can find so pleasurable becomes, at adolescence, something of a mixed blessing.

The Only Child: Mario's Story

Mario referred himself to us when he was 17 on the advice of one of his teachers at his private day school. He wrote a short letter to us saying that he was finding it difficult to concentrate on his A level work. He also mentioned that he was sleeping badly and had been having some bad dreams.

It is our custom in the Adolescent Department to offer a series of four appointments initially. The idea is to create an atmosphere in which the young person is invited to join the therapist in a mutual process of assessment, which is designed to unravel the immediate emotional tensions and to mobilise some new ways of thinking about the problem. It is a simple and straightforward process in which the therapist may ask questions that are so obvious that nobody, including the patient, has thought of asking them before. When I asked Mario 'who is in your

10

family and what is it like at home?' he said he would have to think about it. After a minute or so he said that his parents were Italian and that he was their only child. His parents ran a restaurant and they were very busy. After a few more minutes he added 'they argue quite a lot but the worst thing is that they argue about me'. He looked tense and tearful at that point and I said that he seemed to be experiencing a lot of pressure as if he was in some way to blame for the unhappiness in his family. This seemed to offer him some relief as if it might be possible for him to make sense of his feelings.

In retrospect it did seem important that I had not asked him immediately about the bad dreams he had mentioned in his letter. He came across as a boy who needed space and privacy, so much so that I imagined it had been quite difficult for him to come to the clinic at all. However, in subsequent meetings, and in his own time, he told me about an experience which had been very frightening for him. A business colleague of his father's had been to his house and they had a conversation which had become extremely heated. Mario was in his room watching television. He had heard his mother scream and the front door slamming. His parents had started arguing. Mario heard the Italian words of abuse exchanged between them. He heard his mother cry bitterly. He thought he heard her say 'it's all your fault, you didn't care, you didn't think about me' and then he thought he heard his father say 'why do you talk to your friends about something that is private'. That was all Mario could remember but it was this experience that had led to the bad dreams, dreams which he could not now recall. What Mario did remember was feeling deeply ashamed that he had not gone downstairs to help his parents. That night he had realised that something was terribly wrong, that he was almost afraid of his parents and that deep down he felt he hardly knew them.

This rather mysterious incident was never mentioned again, Mario seemed to want to distance himself from it and I was left simply with Mario's own reflection on the experience which seemed to be a mixture of embarrassment and weariness almost as if he was responsible for these volatile parents.

It was not until much later, after Mario and I had agreed to work together once a week for six months, that he told me about a very significant aspect of his life. He had been born in the Italian countryside when his parents were themselves teenagers. Mario was now the age that his father had been when he was born. When Mario was three years old his parents had, in discussion with other family members, decided to come to England to build a new life, hoping to work hard and become prosperous, both for themselves and also to provide a good life for Mario when he was older. Mario lived with his maternal grandparents in Italy until he was six, when his parents, who visited every summer, took him back to London with them. In London Mario was sent to the best private day schools and it seems was given everything his parents thought that he needed. Every summer holiday he returned to visit his grandparents and sometimes his parents came too when they could free themselves from their work. When I heard that Mario had spent so many early years in Italy I was surprised since he spoke English without any trace of an Italian accent.

One day Mario said to me that he had been thinking that he had been called Mario because it was his birth that led to his parents' marriage. He said this with a wry adolescent smile but nevertheless it helped me to understand the way in which Mario had experienced himself as a child, on the one hand as a very important person 'the centre of their world', on the other hand someone who was 'just born by mistake'. Mario was of course mindful of the fact that it was a 'mistake' that his parents did not make again. Mario said 'if I had younger brothers and sisters my parents certainly wouldn't have the time to keep fussing about my homework'.

It would of course be a cliché to say that all only children are lonely. Many of them, if they are naturally sociable, appreciate the respite from other children in their own home. Mario it seemed had only one 'real friend', another Italian boy of his age.

During this work with Mario I often felt quite sad on the parents' behalf and in this sense felt myself in a rather grandparental role. Clearly Mario was not particularly grateful for his parents' sacrifices. He told me that he thought they worked too hard, that they should go out more to enjoy themselves and furthermore that he was not particularly impressed by his English schoolboy status.

My work with Mario became centred on the separation experiences from the two mother figures early in his life, the loss which had never really been recognised by anybody because the family, understandably, always experienced themselves as always being there for him. An 'extended family in the mind' is a manageable concept for adults but of course for children people are just there or they are not. These issues are often acutely painful for the immigrant and refugee families that we see.

All children are born with different personalities and propensities and some have the capacity to adapt more easily to separations and the challenge of new locations and languages, particularly if there are concerned and loving parental figures to support them. Mario pleased his parents by doing well at school, he conformed but emotionally he could not or would not adapt. His dream was to live in Italy where he told me that he had 'lots of friends'.

In the final two months of our work together Mario was beginning to realise that he had to relinquish some of his resentment and grandiosity. I had been pleased to hear that he had attempted some sort of apology to his parents for his previous reproachful behaviour. Apparently his mother had taken an evening away from the restaurant to talk to Mario about his early life with her and his father. Mario found all this extremely embarrassing and painful but also a relief. In a reflective moment he said to me 'I suppose we are all feeling guilty about something but we couldn't talk about it'. In the following weeks some sort of compromise had been struck. Mario's parents agreed that he could take some special exams which would enable him to go to University in Italy, meeting up with his parents in the holidays.

To put it simply, what Mario had to do was what most of us have to do in order to grow up; that is to relinquish the dream of the childhood we longed for and to acknowledge the reality of the childhood we actually had despite all its shortcomings.

Lone Parents of Adolescents

Traditional and mythical literature is full of warnings about what happens to children who are separated from the idealised, balanced, containing parental couple. Lone parenting is certainly something of a balancing act at the best of times and it would probably be true to say that there are very few single adults who would make the choice to parent adolescents alone, if circumstances did not require them to do so.

There are at least three categories of lone parents: bereaved parents, divorced parents and single parents. Each of these groupings represent distinctly different life experiences and there is understandable indignation when they are treated as one large homogenous group. According to a report from the Office of National Statistics, the number of children living with one parent has trebled since 1972. The figures show that in 1993 nearly 19% of children (more than 2 million) lived with the mother alone and a further 2% with their father alone.

Mrs C requested an appointment at our clinic. She had been divorced for six years and had two children, Carol aged 16 and Peter aged 14. Peter had committed his first serious misdemeanour of adolescence. He

13

had been threatened with suspension from school for setting off a fire alarm as a dare. In the consulting room Mrs C quickly dissolved into tears, feeling that she could not cope; she said she felt helpless. Her daughter Carol, usually very supportive of her mother, had brushed away her worry, saying, 'it's all right mum, it's only a one-off thing'. Peter had said, 'It was just a joke mum, I didn't think about it'. Neither of these laconic adolescent statements consoled her; in fact she experienced her son as becoming shockingly different and felt that he was turning into someone that she did not know.

Peter's father was now living in Kent with a new wife. Mrs C had phoned him asking him to talk to Peter but Peter had refused to go to the phone. Peter had later rebuked his mother with the kind of savagery that adolescents often express when they feel caught out. He said to her, 'It's your problem, you wanted dad to leave this house so why call him now?'

This is a fairly common scenario in lone parent families: a distraught mother, an irritated older sibling and a post pubertal young man testing out the emotional climate. It is not at all unusual for young people to be quite ruthless in their experimentation at this age. When Peter refused to talk to his father on the phone he knew it would make his mother feel distraught and he was beginning to become curious about how much power he might have in the family.

It emerged later that Peter knew from past experience that his mother would not force the issue or threaten him with punishment because he was unconsciously aware that she would then feel identified with her own authoritarian father. In some ways Peter was afraid of his freedom. With hindsight Mrs C could see that it was not a coincidence that Peter had staged his rebellion at school where he would be reprimanded and stopped.

Prior to his adolescence, Mrs C had always managed to persuade Peter to conform by offering him treats or by appealing to his basically kindly nature. Now it seemed this was not enough. Peter needed to know exactly where the boundaries were so that he could feel safe and more in control of his newly experienced strength and vitality. The fact that he could now overrule his mother made him feel both triumphant but also sick with fear. Mrs C and I talked about the fact that she lacked self esteem and that she did not feel that she really had the right to have strong opinions and stick to them.

In an article about female leadership roles at work Lorenzen (1996) says 'personal authority can be defined as a central aspect of self perception ... this concerns the right to exist – to be ones self and to

14

experience authenticity in role ... entitled to act, express points of view and emotions. A person's inner sense of authority will be developed during childhood in the system of family relationships, when the parents express their expectations, ideas, and emotions to their child ... An inhibited person who does not feel that he or she has the right to do very much may not be able to undertake even a minimal amount of role authority. On the other hand, an arrogant person with unrealistic thoughts about their own skills, may execute more authority than the role entitles even in a way that prevents others from undertaking their roles'.

Our therapeutic work with lone parents has a close link with role consultation in the work place. Parenting is after all, a management role, albeit in a highly charged emotional atmosphere. In our experience it is often the case that children are more likely to become aggressive and out of control when they experience their parents as lacking authority and conviction. Parents who feel helpless may lapse into depression or be subject to impulsive displays of aggression out of sheer frustration. In this way an atmosphere of mutual disappointment and recrimination can easily escalate.

In these situations we always try to gather some idea of the availability of extended family members who may be able to help with the resolution of conflicts. The fact that the parent and the therapist are also working and thinking together does itself create or recreate a sense of 'a couple in the mind' which helps to reinforce a sense of integrity in what may have been experienced as an irretrievably broken family.

Mothers and Daughters

'I worry about Molly becoming a clone of me – fearfully competent, comfortably outspoken and yet – where is the freedom for her to make her own mistakes and to be unlike me? If she had a host of brothers and sisters she could try on a variety of roles, but because there is only her and me, the bond between us is tight, almost to snapping point. I'm always consciously trying to give her space. But because there is only one of her, she has to be all things to me. It's a heavy burden.'

Erica Jong, novelist, on her relationship with
her 18-year-old daughter (June 1997).

When a mother and daughter live alone together there is always the possibility of at least a partial merger of identities. While this particular experience of intimacy may offer considerable narcissistic pleasure, security and comfort to both the adult woman and the girl, particularly in the daughter's latency years, it has a tendency to end in tears, especially when one of them becomes emotionally invested elsewhere.

Halberstadt-Freud (1989) in her seminal paper on mother/daughter symbiosis states 'even in normal development, the separation between mothers and daughters seems more problematic than between mothers and sons. The sameness of gender, the resemblances between them and the absence of sexual difference provide ample opportunities for mother and daughter to engage in a mutual identification without separation. Such primary identification prevents the formation of a separate identity and individuality'.

Zoe, aged 17, asked for some counselling. She wrote a very short letter saying that she was feeling under a lot of pressure and couldn't get on with her mother. She said she would like to come and talk to somebody as soon as possible. She had heard about our service from a friend at school.

When I met Zoe she told me that she was an only child, that she had been feeling very anxious and was not sleeping very well. She thought that this was to do with tension between herself and her mother. She then went on to talk about her mother at great length and I heard what an extremely talented person her mother was, a head teacher of a local primary school, much respected by everyone, parents and pupils alike. Zoe herself had been in her mother's class when she was much younger. I commented that she was obviously very proud of her mother and wondered how this might link with the problem that she came here about. Suddenly to my surprise she burst into tears, as if my question had propelled her from nostalgic reverie to the discomfort of the present. I passed Zoe a box of tissues that was on the table between us. She looked at me intensely for a few moments before wiping her tears away with her own hands. I found myself feeling self conscious about the motherly gesture I had made, as if I had acted out of turn, too prematurely and with too much intimacy.

The first few moments of a meeting between strangers are always important but often only understood in retrospect. I realised later that the last thing Zoe wanted from me was a conventionally motherly gesture. She was in fact feeling increasingly imprisoned at home by her mother's constant interest in everything she was doing, particularly her social life. The 'last straw' had been when she discovered that her mother had found out from Zoe's best friend's mother that Zoe had been seeing a boyfriend. Mother had responded to this by leaving a packet of condoms on Zoe's bedside table.

In subsequent meetings Zoe and I tried to understand what was happening between herself and her mother. She had not told her mother that she was coming to see me because 'she would want to know every detail of our conversation'. Despite the fact that Zoe's mother seemed to be acting in an anxious, intrusive way, it seemed to me to be crucially important that I did not collude with Zoe in a criticism of her mother. I needed to be something akin to the absent third member of the family who might have space in the mind for the pain that was being expressed by both mother and daughter.

I recognised a situation which is not unfamiliar in work with adolescents. Sometimes an atmosphere is presented in which a parent seems to be acting like a detective, anxious and alert to the smallest sign of change, the slightest hint or a clue that might be evidence that something is wrong. At the same time an adolescent seems to be reinforcing suspicion by secretive or evasive behaviour. Although everyone seems to be behaving as if a crime is about to be discovered there is in fact no crime, there is merely a situation in which people who have always known each other extremely well, now have to relinquish their right of access to the other and they must learn to bear each other's separateness and privacy. In a very small family this can be experienced as a betrayal.

As Halberstadt-Freud (1989) says 'Separation, implying autonomy, is often already in itself experienced by the girl as disloyalty and as an act of aggression against the mother, even if she does not attack her mother at all in thought or deed. That is because the girl assumes – often rightly – that the mother will experience her daughter's separation as a threat'.

Of course it is not only the parent who may feel the sense of threat. Lone mothers also have a tendency to find new partners and this is sometimes very difficult for adolescents to accept.

It had seemed important to give Zoe time and space to express herself without too many questions from me. However by the sixth meeting there had been no mention of Zoe's father and very little about the boyfriend except for Zoe's outrage that her mother should assume that she was having a sexual relationship when she was not. I realised that Zoe and I were in danger of descending into a boundariless, unthinking, somewhat claustrophobic world, a woman's world of need, in which mother apparently evacuated her anxieties into Zoe and Zoe then came to our session and attempted to evacuate them into me.

However as Zoe came to understand the nature and origins of her feelings of guilt and loss she began to relate to me in a different way. She could now develop some capacity to take a step back into a thinking space in which she could see herself more objectively. I felt that this

17

calmer Zoe could tolerate my asking her about her father and what had happened to him. Zoe's father had been 20 years older than his wife. Zoe's mother had met and married him soon after the long illness and death of the maternal grandmother. Apparently he too was not a well man and his life expectancy was predictably short. He had died when Zoe was six. With my encouragement Zoe brought forth a few ordinary family memories: playing cards with him, singing songs with her mother playing the piano, remembering too that her father had said, some months before he died 'look after your mother'.

Zoe was beginning to experience the mourning that she had never really faced. She was now also aware that her mother's own mourning was incomplete in some way, as if mother had simply transferred an intense pre-occupation with her own mother first to her husband and subsequently to her young daughter.

Zoe continued in therapy for a further year. It was also decided to offer Zoe's mother some help in her own right as a parent. The idea was that this would help both mother and daughter to gradually disentangle their emotions and to begin to tolerate more space and separateness.

Keeping the Absent Father in Mind

'Father Away'

Derek, age 16, whose parents were divorced told me that he had a special nickname for his father. He called him 'father away'. He seemed very pleased with this adolescent pun, telling me that occasionally he even referred to his father as 'away' for short. Once, a few weeks later he referred to a weekend visit to his father and step-mother as an 'away game'. In fact Derek had missed his father very much and had been furious about what he experienced as his parents' incapacity to live together. His jokes and puns with their obvious associations to football did seem to help him to keep a link with his father, and their mutual interest in sport, at a time when it was very difficult for father and son to discuss their feelings about the separation.

Although Derek reproached his father with the 'away' label he did in fact manage to see his father quite often. 'In my case' he said 'father away' is also 'father down the road'. Of course it is harder for children whose parents' new marital arrangements take them away not only from fathers but also from friends and familiar places. The pain of this was dramatically evident in Mario's story.

Many of the young people who use our services are in a situation where their biological parents are living in separate places and most of them live with their mothers. Many of these small families fall into the 'father down the road' category where there is a certain amount of regular contact.

The Father in the Mind

There are also a considerable number of children who have never known their fathers and in these cases their mother's mental relationship to the lost partner is crucial, particularly if the circumstances around the child's birth were unplanned or unhappy. For a boy the status of the 'father in the mother's mind' will inevitably reflect on his own sense of masculine identity and worth. If there is no internalised experience of a once loved or loveable father, boys are in danger of making superficial kinds of masculine identifications based on imitation and stereotype. For girls it seems to be more of a question of whether mother was experienced as loveable in the eyes of the unknown father. In the absence of factual history the girl is liable to be overcome by fantasies of a protective, even heroic father, and this can lead to a romantic idealisation which may dangerously edge towards a passive, masochistic state of mind.

Secrets

It is in adolescence that a curiosity, often latent for many years, will begin to emerge. Direct questions will be asked about the genesis and the nature of the original parental relationship. Single mothers often ask for guidance in what for them is an extremely difficult and delicate task; to be truthful about the past and at the same time to spare the adolescent and themselves from unnecessary pain.

Angelica Garnett, the daughter of Venessa Bell, has written poignantly about the revelation of her father's identity in her adolescence. For 17 years she and her brothers had been living with Vanessa and Clive Bell and a family friend and fellow artist Duncan Grant.

> One day ... Vanessa ... took me into the drawing room at Charleston and told me that Duncan, not Clive was my real father. She hugged me close and spoke about love; underneath her sweetness of manner lay an embarrassment and a lack of ease of which I was acutely aware and which washed over my head like the waves of the sea.

Later she looks back at the situation from the adult point of view.

19

So absolute was my confidence in their wisdom that I never thought of blaming either Duncan or Vanessa for their silence. Even later when my resentment fell upon Vanessa, I never could bring myself to blame Duncan. This was years afterwards when I had begun to realise what I had missed and how deeply the ambiguity of the situation had sunk into me...

Although Vanessa comforted herself with the pretence that I had two fathers, in reality – emotional reality that is – I had none. It was impossible to associate Duncan with any idea of paternity – and he never tried to assume such a role. Clive acted better but carried no conviction, for he knew the truth. How different it would be if we had all acknowledged it.

Angelica Garnett's story came strongly to my mind when a general practitioner referred a 14 year old girl, Adelle, who had taken an overdose after discovering that her older sister was actually her mother and the people she had always thought of as her parents were in fact her grandparents. She had heard this in a shockingly sudden manner from a cousin who was not much older than herself and she was quite unable to cope with the consequences at this vulnerable time of her developing identity. Adelle needed to spend some time in a special adolescent unit where she was carefully looked after and where her wider family were given support to begin to understand Adelle's state of shock and the enormity of her grief and confusion. When some understanding could be tolerated several members of the extended family were very useful to Adelle in helping her to gently piece together her personal history.

Secrets can become even more insidious in a very small family where risking a revelation may also be risking the stability of the only close relationship you have.

The Oblique Art of Adolescent Communication

In conclusion I would like to touch on two significant themes that were highlighted in the introduction; these are the adolescent tendency to mystification and the restorative influence of humour.

A Dialogue of Approximation

Generally speaking the pre-teenage child is concerned with the small and reliable certainties of his or her everyday life. There is an interest in rules and routines, sometimes to the extent of their being rather superior and fastidious in relation to their parents' habits or the way the household is managed. Naturally parents are surprised when these rather exact and exacting young people start to speak like this: 'My friend goes like you know there's this party and stuff and I sort of want to go but it doesn't really bother me you know what I mean and I'm thinking like why not, it might be a laugh or whatever'.

For a while I was so accustomed to this kind of dialogue from young people at work, at home and on the television that I failed to notice what was so distinctive about it. It is in fact almost a language of its own, a multi-cultural user-friendly pidgin in which there are limitless possibilities to express desire without commitment. It is a language of identity-in-flux.

Reading the T-shirts

Despite all the difficulty, the misunderstandings, the fear and indeed the hatred that can be felt and expressed between parents and adolescents there comes a time when somewhat to their surprise they find themselves sharing a joke. This will be a particularly new kind of joke, quite distinct from adolescent pseudo-cynicism or the parental ridicule of earlier times. This is the joke that recognises the absurdities of life, the positions and postures and poses that have been taken up during the mutual obstinacies of battle.

These moments of unpredictable and spontaneous amnesty are personal to every family. A therapist is unlikely to hear about the content of the joke nor would she understand it. She can only be aware that something has moved and that expressions of irony, affection and lightness are more in evidence in the patient.

Nearer to the end of his therapy Mario arrived wearing an unusual T-shirt. It seemed to depict a large washing machine with bizarre objects whizzing around inside it. I wondered if Mario would comment on this but he did not, having other more important things to tell me. This was the week that his parents had agreed that he could go to University in Italy and join his Italian friends there. Later as Mario turned to go he walked slowly to the door. On the back of his T-shirt were the words JOHN FELT LIKE A LOST SOCK IN THE LAUNDROMAT OF OBLIVION. Having given me just enough time to read it he left with a wry smile.

I thought that Mario knew that I would understand that self parody was somewhere on the road to self understanding and the capacity to let go of grievance.

21

Zoe too had a T-shirt which she sometimes wore when she came to see me. Hers said LACK OF CHARISMA CAN BE FATAL. Again it wasn't something that we needed to discuss directly since I knew how much Zoe longed to feel that she could be appreciated for her own qualities rather than be simply needed by somebody. As with Mario the T-shirt was some sort of gentle parody of her own fears and once again it demonstrated an ironic stance which Zoe needed to think clearly and objectively about herself. I am told that the most popular T-shirt of all refers to the first album of a famous British rock band. It simply reads DEFINITELY MAYBE and as far as adolescents are concerned you cannot get clearer than that.

References

Lorenzen, Z. (1996) 'Female leadership: some parental and professional reflections', in *The Leadership and Organization Development Journal*, 6.

Jong, E. (1997) 'Growing up, growing old, growing closer', *Independent on Sunday*, 8 June 1997.

Halberstadt-Freud, H.C. (1989) 'Electra in bondage', *Free Associations*, 17: 58-89.

Garnett, A. (1984) *Deceived with Kindness: A Bloomsbury Childhood*, Oxford University Press.

2

'How Does It Work Here, Do We Just Talk?'

Therapeutic Work with Young People Who Have Been Sexually Abused

Stephen Briggs

Of all the forms of trauma which can be visited upon young people, sexual abuse, either occurring in adolescence or 'remembered' during the process of adolescent development, is one of the most poignant, painful; and, from the therapist's point of view, difficult to treat. The therapist inevitably has to work both with the reality of the external events, the trauma itself, with issues of protection, which bring him/her into contact with the Child Protection requirements, and the network of professionals in this field.

When young people who have been abused seek therapeutic help, whether the actual abuse is incest, abuse within the wider family, or abuse which takes place in the context of 'risk taking' behaviour outside the family, there is always a need to consider a complex history of disturbing and difficult relationships affecting the young person. Treating the consequences of abuse means both trying to understand the impact of the trauma on the young person, and also understanding the qualities of the experiences the individual has known throughout life, and the way these have been taken in, or internalised, to become the relationships which hold significance in the internal world.

In this chapter I wish to explore three themes which occur in working with young people who have been abused. First, I shall focus on the problem of beginning a therapeutic relationship at the point of disclosure of abuse and the impact of this on both therapist and young person. Second, I shall discuss the problems that arise in terms of the young person developing a sense of identity, and how this emerges in the therapeutic relationship. Thirdly, I shall suggest some ways in which the young person begins the process of recovery, through a discussion of the idea of resilience. To illustrate all three themes I shall draw on therapeutic work I undertook over three years with a young woman who had been abused for a substantial period of time, in her early teens.

Crossing the Boundary: Beginning a Therapeutic Relationship at the Point of Disclosing Sexual Abuse

The beginning of therapy for any young person marks a complex psycho-social transition from a private, familial and peer context for discussing difficulties and seeking emotional support, to a more public, professional domain. Both therapist and client have intense hopes, fears and expectations prior to meeting (Wittenberg, 1970). When the young person has been sexually abused, the therapist has also to be aware of the tension between the aim to establish a confidential, safe and supportive environment for the young person, and the responsibilities as a professional to prevent abuse, through contact with other professionals. This tension can affect the therapist's openness to the communications of the young person, and he/she is vulnerable to being pulled or nudged, either towards denying the abuse, its seriousness and its implications, or, at the other end of this spectrum, to becoming over actively involved in discovering, and rooting out, 'the truth'. (Steiner, 1985; 1993) Neither of these extremes are, of course, helpful, but it is often difficult to respond to the many layers of communication presented by a young person seeking professional help. He or she may be unsure of what she wants from the therapy, of what therapy is or will mean to him or her. The young person may present a kaleidoscope of differing wishes and fears at the beginning of therapeutic contact; the fear of being further harmed, and the wish to be rid of all the pain and damage are commonly present, and these are both described by Wittenberg (1970).

Additionally, when the therapist is male, and the therapist and young person come from different cultural backgrounds, the anticipated fears, hopes and expectations embrace striking issues of difference. Cultural difference increases the fear that there will be a lack of or misunderstanding, originating from a history of prejudice, which reaches all levels of social communication, including fairy tales, images, myths and jokes (Thomas, 1992). Racism and sexual abuse share as an essential part of their dynamics an abuse of power. There is the possibility of 'a simple re-enactment of other social scenarios' (Thomas, 1992, p. 136), in that the (white) therapist can assume superiority over the (black) client. In these circumstances, Thomas suggests it is the therapists task

24

'to recognise and explore pathological fit along racial lines in the transference'. (Thomas, ibid., 136).

There has been considerable debate as to whether male therapists should see female victims of abuse. Frosh (1987) suggests that male therapists should not be involved in the early stages of disclosure of female victims. Mann (1989) writing specifically about incest by the father suggests that, on the contrary, the male therapist can redefine the role of relationships with men, based on non-abusive experience. I would suggest that the main arguments against male therapists working with sexually abused young people stem from clinical considerations; first, following the approach of Casement (1985), the therapist should learn from the female patient whether she can bear to work on these issues with a man. Second, and I shall return to this theme later, the viability of work with a male therapist depends on the patient having a capacity to make use of symbolic forms of communication, rather than turning words into things, in a very concrete way, in the way Segal describes symbol equation (1957). In this framework, it is an important task of an assessment to discover and evaluate the possibility for therapeutic help on an individual basis.

This is not as simple a task as I may have suggested. Inevitably, the early phases of a therapeutic meeting in these circumstances, that is, of abuse, are laden with multiple levels of meaning and communication. In the example from my own work that I have in mind, where the young person had been sexually abused, and where the differences between us included gender, race as well as generation, the task of assessment was illustrative of these complex processes at work.

Freud (1909b, p. 160) wrote that the first communications of a patient hold special importance. Alvarez (1992, p. 15) adds that this is so, if only we have the wit and understanding to see it.[1] In this example, far from having 'wit and understanding' I felt myself to be in a tense dilemma, which I shall try to describe:

On the first occasion I met her, C, a petite young woman, wearing a loose fitting top and jeans, looked at me with an eager smile which seemed to dispel any sense that she may be anxious. She clutched tightly the letter I had sent her offering her this meeting. She said she is '18, nearly 18 and she lives in an extended family', and added that 'he' is there a lot of the time, and 'he' is part of her extended family. Speaking quickly, she said that she had almost forgotten about it, or really forgot about it for some time. She stopped speaking abruptly and again looked at me. She said that she 'knew I would want to know all the details'.

I felt at the time that this was an extraordinarily condensed series of

25

statements about herself. I was struck by the rhythm of her speech; the powerfully constricted space containing so many facts and ideas; the abruptness of her ending and the directness of her statement that 'she knew I would want to know all the details'.

Her appearance was more that of a latency child than a young woman; her eager smile betrayed a wish, perhaps, to cover her anxiety, and to placate me; her comment about the extended family intimated her different cultural background that was mentioned indirectly, conveying a feeling that I might not understand, Hearing 'all the details' could well have constituted a re-enactment of a pattern of racial and even racist dynamics, in which I became a 'superior' authority to whom she submitted. In truth, the dilemma was an acute one; to hear these 'details' amounted to a fraught possibility. To do so would immediately turn the therapeutic relationship into one which in a sense transgressed boundaries; usually one might expect to get to know the young person first. Second, it had the potential to sexualise the meeting, and third, it presented me as a man who might wish to hear about sexual details. Yet not to hear what had happened to her, when, as she said, she had nearly 'forgotten' about it, when she was now ready to talk to someone after years of silence, was also not satisfactory. I would in this case be on the side of those who did not want to know, and could not bear to hear what it is she has to say, and what has happened to her. In this dilemma, and the strength of the opposites – immediate disclosure of all the details to not being heard – lay her expectations of relationships. In this sense, and in the way she described her social circumstances – being nearly 18, on the point of adulthood, she did indeed convey a great deal about herself in these first communications.

I decided that the emphasis of my response should be placed on the context of our very new contact; she had so recently crossed the boundary into the clinic. I said to her that I felt she had the sense that she had important things to tell me, that she ought to tell me these things, but that it was a lot to say so soon. I also sensed that she was uncomfortable about talking to me. She said she was keen to come here, she has heard this is a good place, but she knew it would take years to sort this out.

Her belief that she would need a long time appears as a fearful expectation, and her wish to talk straight away about the details of her abuse seemed therefore more like a wish to pre-empt the processes of engaging in a relationship with someone over a long period of time. It also suggested a pessimism, about problems she had which were really intractable, or deep, or both. Here there was another unknown, which

26

she verbalised almost immediately; how does she talk to a man, who is different and 'other', and how does this talking help her. 'How does it work here?', she asked me, looking directly at me, 'Do we just talk?' Is it possible, one might add, that there can be a relationship which is 'just talk' without transgressing boundaries, and at the same time, how anxious that prospect can make someone in her situation.

I did experience some relief in myself that in taking this path out of the dilemma about hearing or not 'all the details', it was possible to talk more directly about the thoughts and feelings she had on beginning this contact with me, and in particular to think about what it meant for her to talk to me across the cultural and gender boundaries. She told me that she had been unhappy when she realised the appointment letter was from a man, but she had shown her older sister who had said that she could have a 'good experience'(sic) and this would overcome her fear. When she left at the end of the first session she said 'that was quite nice' and in an almost subtle way I felt there was a barely conscious sexualisation of being in a room with me. The quality of space in the room was saturated with sexuality, with the backing, so to speak, of the sister who encouraged her to have a good experience and her mother, who, C told me, forgave the cousin who abused her. C herself expected to be coming to see me for years, but, when I suggested she might have some doubts about this she said she hoped it would be 'all done' in one session, hence the need to get 'all the details' out, and left with me. She, however, felt really that she could not forget, nor simply run away. Again I felt I had to find some space between this 'all or nothing', coming for years or getting it 'all done' in one meeting, and I suggested we met for up to four times, to establish how we could work together.

During the first few meetings with C I always had a sense of ambiguity within her communications, in that there was both a genuine communication about her situation and her relationship with me, and also a quality of a physical, sexual, concrete communication. These two levels of communication appeared to run alongside each other, in parallel, as also occurs in young people with eating disorders (Briggs, 1995). While it was clear that there was a capacity to relate at a symbolic level, and that this made it possible to work with her and speak to her about her feelings and experiences in her therapy, the presence of the concrete, physical level of experiencing my communications left me feeling very cautious about how I took up with her what she said. I was unsure whether to address issues in relationship to me, in the transference, because of the risk of her experiencing this in a concrete or literal way. In particular, this affected, discussing issues about the abuse and

27

her sexuality directly. Not only did I not hear 'the details' but it became impossible to speak directly about sexuality, for these communications might have been taken very concretely by her.

In retrospect I feel that this inhibition led me to be too cautious, not so much with regard to talking about sexuality, but rather with regard to discussing her deeper anxieties. When I was able to free myself enough to say something about how she might be experiencing me, a deeper sense of emotional contact occurred.[2] For example, in the fifth session she spoke in a way that suggested she had a string of complaints. Firstly, she said that her abuser should be made to leave the family home. She was indeed concerned with the prospects that if her father got to know about the abuse, it was not clear who would be punished; it may be her abuser or it may be her. However, she also added that she thought I was just doing a job, and that I was not interested in her really. This gave me the opportunity to speak to her about her sense that there was something missing for her in her experience of my attention to her, and some mistrust therefore of whether I would allow her to stay in her therapy. The problem of trust was central to her current difficulties, to her sense of identity and her capacity for action in her world.

A similar example occurred in the seventh meeting when she spoke in a confused and confusing way of her anxiety about someone she had met whom she would like to be a boyfriend. I had the strong sense that this was a communication about me as well as the young man she was thinking of. She said she could not concentrate and she forgave her abuser. I commented that she really did seem confused and she replied immediately that she was frightened. She was frightened of her potential boyfriend, her uncle and her father. I asked if that applied to me too. She said, not so much, but then she added that she just remembered that she was very frightened on coming to the door of my room. She could not understand it, but it was there.

Some of her reluctance to connect the experiences with her family and with me stemmed from the inter-cultural context of this relationship. C said that she had 'no problem' with seeing a white person, and 'all her friends are white'. There was within her a propensity to split between a 'good' outside and a 'bad' family, and that I would be safer, in the short term, if I could be seen as part of her friendship network. I could be a 'friend' and thus kept more distant than the intimate – and confused – relationships within her family. Later when she spoke in more detail of the abuse I was to learn that her anxiety at the door of my room was a re-enactment of her experiences of going to the door of her abuser.

28

In fact C was becoming more attached to her therapy, and more valuing of it. In this way she was establishing the position of temporary outsidership in her family (Dartington, 1994), and from this position she became slightly more detached. Because of this it became possible for the extent of the abuse within the family to be known, and acted upon in terms of the community, the legal and child protection domains. Her therapy then became for a time a place where she sought support and encouragement (meaning literally instilling courage) for her decisions to tell the police what happened to her, to tell her father, and for the siblings to know about – consciously – what happened to them all. She was very active in these processes, though there was also a shared aspect to this work, in which the Department made contact with the relevant professionals and this was discussed with her.[3]

The meeting of the aims in the legal domain – the abuse ending, perpetrators being known, victims compensated – was closely linked with the development of a containing therapeutic space, in which her abuse was not forgotten, but thought about. However, the process stirred up a striking mixture of relief and guilt for C. All the 'details' did in fact become told – but, at this point in time, to a WPC, and not to me.

I have emphasised that in this process of disclosure issues of race and gender in the therapeutic relationship contributed to the fragility and tension in the relationship. I found I had to work very hard, moving in my mind between different levels of meaning with almost all C's communications. I was helped in this work by her capacity to remain a temporary outsider with regard to her family and her anxieties about becoming an 'outcast' were to an extent contained. In this way she showed a capacity to make use of the therapeutic process. I have suggested that this was because she was able to make use of a thinking space, to consider her experiences symbolically, and I should add that there did seem from early on qualities in her relationship with her father that she brought to her therapy. She had loving feelings for her father, and also feared him, feared his knowledge of the abuse, and feared for him,[4] that it would damage or kill him to know about it. Her positive feelings for her father were transferred to me (as was her fear of him, as I have described) and as such helped the formation of the relationship with me. Resolving her relationship with both her paternal and maternal figures was a quest in which we became deeply involved; a quest which can be considered as her development of a sense of identity.

Questions of Identity: The Effects of Abuse in the Adolescent Process

It was a significant moment in the work with C when she told me that her father had been told of the abuse. She was not excluded from the family, as she had feared, and her father had tearfully embraced her and taken upon himself the responsibility for the abuse happening. However, though this increased her sense of trust and security for the moment, the problems for which the abuse was both cause and consequence continued and therapeutic work with C continued for a further two and a half years.

Having traumatic and damaging experiences at the time of puberty affected C's sense of identity. It was a difficult process for her to gain an integrated sense of herself in these circumstances and her difficulties had connections with both the major transitions of adolescence. The trauma of abuse occurred during and after puberty, the first transition. The need emanating from within her to make these experiences known occurred as she reached the increasingly long,[5] second transition from adolescent dependence on the family to adult independence and separateness. Briefly, I shall describe three themes which were relevant to her sense of identity; her experiences of the transition to puberty, making links between opposites, and her relationship with her body.

An aspect of the turmoil of her transition from childhood to adolescence was illustrated by a dream, which she told me after nearly a year of therapy:

'She was in a lift in which she regularly travels. On this occasion it travelled as usual, floor by floor, until it reached the 12th floor. Then it took off, exploding upwards and she was fearful both that it would not stop and that it would crash to earth'.

The understanding we came to share about this dream was that each floor represented a year of her life; the 12th floor related to the onset of puberty, which began when she was 11. After puberty, the gradual progress, floor by floor, or year by year, was replaced with a violent explosiveness. C's experience of the transition from childhood to adolescence was then explosive, fearful and catastrophic. That she travelled in a lift to her sessions also linked the dream with her fear of seeing me, which she felt as she approached the door of my room. the dream also had an obvious phallic imagery, as though she were in identification with the phallus. It also suggested an underlying, infantile

30

disturbance, in which she was not held, but was falling apart (Bick, 1968; Winnicott, 1974).

Her difficulty with the transition to puberty, compounded and triggered by the abuse led to an intensified mistrust in the adult world. In herself, as seen in the way she looked and dressed, she had retreated to the world of childhood, before puberty. The adult world was seen as a perverse and monstrous place, but now she was reaching adulthood herself, she knew she needed to resume contact with this world. Another dream she had vividly illustrates this:

> C said she had a dream 2 days ago. She had a strong sense of urgency to tell me. She was in their old house, which they left when she was 13. It was like the old house, but not like it. It was run down, and dilapidated and unused. She was an adult in a girl's body, and upstairs. Downstairs there were sounds of prostitution taking place. She could not find a way of getting down there. It was like looking through a window. There was a spiral staircase. Somehow she found herself downstairs, not knowing how she got there. There were rooms with numbers; 13, 14. and she knew she must not go in there. Then she found herself face to face with three witch like women with spiky hair sticking out. She felt relief that she had got there.

We spent considerable time thinking about this dream, which features perverse sexuality, prostitution, witches with spiky hair and her being a woman in a girl's body. This was how she would have experienced herself in the abuse, aged 13 and 14, and how she experienced herself now; unable to move into the adult world. She felt she did want to have boyfriend relationships but she was very anxious about any form of closeness, particularly physical closeness. Now she seemed anxious not to be left stranded as an adult in a girl's body. But to go downstairs meant entering a frightening and perverse world.

In the course of discussing the dream, the details of the abuse became known, and named. At 13/14 she was unable to become curious about her mother's sexuality, and what happened in her mother's 'room'. As a substitute for this involvement with her mother, and as a means of retreating from the anxieties she had about identifying with a depressed, damaged and abused mother, she went into another room, with her abusing cousin. The consequences were that she had become traumatically stuck in her development.

She added to the dream that:

> She went up and downstairs several times, and that the house was like it had bits stuck on to it rather than having staircases which were 'integral'.

31

This indicated both the lack of integration – as exemplified by the body and mind being incongruous, and also the difficulty of making connections between parts of the self which would suggest a lack of resilience, and being stuck. I made a comment about the difficulty of linking the upstairs (thinking) with the downstairs (her feelings). She asked how I got there? I said, as in the dream I came from 'upstairs' to downstairs' without her knowing how, and thus threatening her sense of control.

Her curiosity ('how did I get there?') and her wish to know about herself helped her to face the issues she needed to understand, in order to establish an identity as a person, a woman, and indeed a black woman. Curiosity about my thinking restarted a process of curiosity which she had turned away from when she was 13/14. In this process, opposites, such as thinking and feeling, girl and woman, intimacy and distance, being with and being separate needed to be tolerated. How she could relate to my capacity, as she experienced it, to move between different levels of things, from upstairs to downstairs, became a focus of her attempt to integrate these experiences. This sense of identity began with her sense of her body.

Recovery: The Development of Resilience and a Capacity to Separate

Trust, the capacity to rely on an internal experience of love and protection, is shattered by trauma, and slowly reclaimed in therapeutic work. When, as in C's case, the trauma was abuse which itself indicated both the level of family dysfunction and infantile disturbance, trust may never have been established and the capacity for resilience more difficult to achieve. I have seen in infants how the capacity for resilience arises from the capacity to make connections between different levels of experience, to express and symbolise earlier anxieties and experiences in play and words (Briggs, 1997). Resilience also requires the capacity to have faith in a good object (Britton, 1997) and the courage to repeatedly risk the turmoil of newness, for the sake of understanding and integration. C did have a sense of a 'good object' which she concretely described to me as the repeated grip on her father's hand as she went to sleep; that she would reach out to hold him again, and he was able to stay with her. She did not seem, as some others who have been sexually abused, or indeed subject to severe trauma of any kind, to be lacking in any kind of notion of a good object. The fact that her parents were not her sexual abusers helped immeasurably, despite the chronic chaos of her family. For C the development of resilience meant a kind of healing, as she put it, and again became discussible between us through reflections on her dreams: she said she had a dream about watering a plant. She had wanted a plant for a long time and she wanted to put it in her room. In her dream the plant had a deep cut near the roots, not going all the way through but it was deep. She had to hold on to it all the time to support it. I asked what she made of the dream and she said 'a lot' (this said with emphasis).She thought the plant was her and the cut near the root meant she had experienced the cut a long time ago, at the time of her abuse.

There has emerged something within her which enables her to support herself, though this is difficult, and the deep cut means the plant will remain at risk unless it is continually looked after. There is in fact a sense of inner protectiveness towards herself, which Melanie Klein (1957) described as 'an object which loves and protects the self, and is loved and protected by the self'.

In fact the cut is near to the beginning. She was premature, born weighing 2 lbs, and spent a long time in an incubator. Her difficulty in tolerating separateness, in the sense of losing physical contact with another, related to an internal terror of falling, crashing and exploding that she recalled in the lift dream. She only just survived birth and infancy; the cut was deep. Being alone was something she could not bear. This played its part in her risk taking behaviour, since she maintained the relationship, and sometimes sought contact with the abuser. C loathed dependency, and the vulnerability that went with it. This focused on the denigration of her mother – herself an abused woman. C said she 'hated mother love'. If she went close to mother she found herself cringing with disgust, as though she was being contaminated by the contact, and this recalled her image of the 'ditch'. In her relationship with me she was both very dependent and troubled by this dependency. She was totally ashamed of times when she cried. When not denying her dependent feelings, she was quite depressed, particular when there was a break in our work. I was not only a male and white, and 'other' figure, but also a 'maternal' figure she wanted to be close to but felt contaminated by. She fought against the maternal transference in order to keep to minimum the times she felt like this; vulnerable and contaminated.

Limitations in the capacity to develop resilience were connected with her difficulties in facing and tolerating being separate. This had a root in her relationship with both parents – in which opposites were combined. It stirred up for her difficulties in triadic relationships, in which

33

there was desire, hatred of being alone, and intolerance of a parental couple with regard to which she was on the outside. This constellation is described by Britton (1989) as the third position. Again, this material was discussed in the context of the dreams she brought to her therapy, but alongside the relative richness of the imagery of her dreams, was a real sense of emptiness, a terrible fear of being alone, and of not being liked or wanted. She brought so many dreams because she hated the times there was silence in the room, and she related this hatred of silence to the times at home when there was no one there, and the memory, recalled in detail, of when the abuse took place.

We had many discussions about her difficulties with her relationships, especially when there was an intimation from friends, family or acquaintances of feelings of attraction towards her. At these times she would sit as far away from me as possible, her coat wrapped around her. She wished to express her own desires, and to feel important and loved, but she experienced travelling into these realms to be an ordeal she could not bear.

Related to these difficult feelings was her inability to tolerate being alone. She accomplished this with much misery, and also through becoming identified with an image of me in which she believed I spent time I was not with her in a kind of feverish and distraught studying. This was the mirror of how she spent her time, particularly in the last year of the therapy when she was preparing for exams. Her capacities to think and work were adversely affected by the problems she had in being alone, and the inability to tolerate silence, which meant, I think, an awareness of very persecutory sounds within her, preventing her having any space to think. Her pain in this respect became much greater if she began to think of me as someone who was separate from her, and who had relationships with other people. When this difference between us became apparent, some work became possible, in a slow and agonised way, with regard to her separateness and her capacity to tolerate her own position in the world. It was provocative to her to think that I could be engaged with someone else in my mind and not have her as part of that relationship. She was outside this 'coupling' of myself and another, observing it, and finding it painful, as her omnipotent attempts to control me began to fail. This was the other side of 'outsidership', that she felt excluded from something important to her, and it was painful to be so excluded.

Conclusion

In work with young people who have been abused it is necessary to face up to the impact upon the individual of the effects of trauma. Even the word trauma, perhaps through its repeated usage, fails to convey the quality of the difficulties faced by the individual who has suffered abuse. In therapeutic work, both the therapist and the young person must attempt to work with a range of difficult emotions, expressed in complex ways in the therapeutic relationship. The complexity and delicacy of the qualities of the relationship are heightened by issues of difference, which I have illustrated in this case through race and gender.

It is important not to idealise the therapeutic process, to think, for example, that the effects of abusive relationships are 'overcome' by this work. Alvarez comments that 'we should not be surprised to find the abuse still plays a part even in the healthiest of symbolisations' (1992, p. 162). Realistically, in the case example I have used there was evidence that the therapeutic relationship offered a space for the young person in which thinking and integration could begin to take place, and be sustained over time. In particular, the containing process of the therapeutic relationship brings together the young person's needs to 'remember' and to find internal resources which enable negotiation of the emotionally powerful transitions of adolescence.

Notes

1. Alvarez adds that 'it is difficult to be a microscope and a telescope at one and the same time', a view with which I can fully concur, both as a therapist in this situation and in trying to write about a subject which has relevance for both broad, socially important issues, and the emotional experiences in the consulting room.

2. This is close to Steiner's (1993) discussion of 'analyst centred interpretations'.

3. Though I have considered the aspect of contact between professionals briefly, I do not underestimate its importance. Here, I was in the fortunate position of, firstly, working with someone who was not currently being abused, and in a team where a colleague undertook the work across the 'boundary' of the Clinic. Preservation of the therapeutic space for C could be treated as paramount, and not only took into account her wishes on the subject but recognised that she was an adult. Work with younger, less competent and co-operative young people in this way is inevitably more difficult. At times, the need for the abuse to be known is the absolute priority.

4. Freud (1909a) describes Little Hans having the same combination of feelings for his father; fearing and fearing for him.

35

5. See, for example, Furlong and Cartmel (1997) for a summary of the social trends which lengthen the process of transition to adulthood.

References

Alvarez, A. (1992) *Live Company*, London: Routledge.

Bick, E. (1968) 'The experience of the skin in early object relations', in *International Journal of Psychoanalysis*, 49: 484-6.

Briggs, S. (1995) 'Parallel process: emotional and physical digestion in adolescents with eating disorders', *Journal of Social Work Practice*, 9 (2): 155-68.

—— (1997) *Growth and Risk in Infancy*, London: Jessica Kingsley.

Britton, R. (1989) 'The Missing Link: Parental Sexuality in the Oedipus Complex', in R. Britton, C. Feldman and E. O'Shaughnessy (eds), *The Oedipus Complex Today*, London: Karnac.

—— (1997) 'Psychic reality and unconscious belief: a reply to Harold B. Gerard', *International Journal of Psychoanalysis*, 78: 335-9.

Casement, P. (1985) *On Learning from the Patient*, London: Tavistock.

Dartington, A. (1994) 'Some Thoughts on the Significance of the Outsider in Families and Other Social Groups', in S. Box, B. Copley, J. Magagna, E. Moustaka (eds) *Crisis in Adolescence: Object Relations Therapy with the Family*, Washington: Aronson.

Freud, S. (1909a) 'Analysis of a Phobia in a Five Year Old Boy', (Little Hans), *S.E.*, 3, London: Hogarth.

—— (1909b) 'Notes Upon a Case of Obsessional Neurosis', (The Ratman), *S.E.*, 10, p. 155, London: Hogarth.

—— (1917) 'Mourning and Melancholia', *S.E.*, 14, p. 239, London: Hogarth.

Frosh, S. (1987) 'Issues for men working with sexually abused children', *British Journal of Psychotherapy*, 3 (4): 332-9.

Furlong, A. and Cartmel, F. (1997) *Young People and Social Change*, Open University Press.

Klein, M. (1957) *Envy and Gratitude*, repr. in M. Klein (1988) *Envy and Gratitude and Other Works, 1946-63*, London: Virago.

Mann, D. (1989) 'Incest: the father and the male therapist', *British Journal of Psychotherapy*, 6 (2): 143-53.

Segal, H. (1957) 'Notes on symbol formation', *International Journal of Psychoanalysis*, 38: 391-7.

Steiner, J. (1985) 'Turning a blind eye: the cover up for Oedipus', *International Review of Psychoanalysis*, 12: 161-72.

—— (1993) *Psychic Retreats*, London: Routledge.

Thomas, L. (1992) 'Racism and Psychotherapy: Working with Racism in the Consulting Room – An Analytic View', in J. Kareem and R. Littlewood *Intercultural Therapy: Themes, Interpretations and Practice*, London: Blackwell Scientific Publications.

Winnicott, D.W. (1974) 'Fear of breakdown', *International Review of Psychoanalysis*, 1 (1): 103-7.

Wittenberg, I. (1970) *Psychoanalytic Insights and Relationships*, London: Routledge.

3

Psychotherapy with Learning Disabled Adolescents

Lynda Miller

When referrals of learning disabled young people with emotional difficulties are received by the adolescent department, they are usually assessed and treated by a psychotherapist from the Tavistock Clinic's Learning Disability Service, which specialises in therapeutic work with learning disabled patients of all ages.

Traditionally, the learning disabled have been those with a measured IQ below 70, and who have usually been educated in special schools. However, definitions of learning disability vary and can be related to social and emotional factors. Those young people who have emotional problems in conjunction with a learning disability may respond well to a psychotherapeutic approach.

I want to consider some factors that I think are of particular significance in therapeutic work with adolescents who have learning disabilities of varying degrees of severity. These factors include sexuality, restriction of independent mobility, and very low self esteem. I suggest that the question of the extent to which these young people experience themselves as different from their non-disabled peers underlies the therapeutic work, and that the issue of sameness and difference appears in a variance of forms according to the seriousness and the nature of the disability.

A useful distinction can perhaps be made between those cases where the learning disability is moderate and not visibly obvious, and those where it is severe and visible. There can of course be overlap between these two categories, for example a person with Down's Syndrome or a physical disability, and a moderate learning disability. The therapeutic work tends to have a different emphasis in each of these categories and I will illustrate these points with case material later.

One can also speculate as to whether external factors such as sexual

37

abuse, deprivation, neglect or a more subtle failure in the parent-child relationship may have contributed to the young person's learning disability. This is likely to be so, but the extent to which these factors are causative is a complex issue. In cases where there is no known genetic or organic disorder one gains in the course of the therapeutic work an idea of the relevance of these factors to the learning disability.

In the referrals of adolescents with Down's Syndrome and other genetic or organic disorders, external factors may also be contributory to the young person's emotional and learning difficulties. However, the learning disability is clearly integral to the personality and gives rise to recognisable forms of mental functioning. As such, undertaking psychotherapy with a perhaps severely learning disabled adolescent is a fascinating if difficult task. As a therapist, one has to free oneself from pre-conceptions and focus upon the nature of the relationship which unfolds in the weekly sessions over time, between patient and therapist. Gradually, one gains insight into the internal world of the patient and has the task of trying to understand and to explore the ways in which development can unfold.

Learning disabled adolescents, like all young people, have defences which have built up over time to protect the emergent self. However, too rigid or too massive defences will be stifling to the growth of the personality. As we all know, learning disabled young people are highly vulnerable in society and are all too often subjected to experiences which they find threatening or frightening. They will almost invariably have found ways to defend themselves against anxieties and these can be studied in the context of the therapeutic relationship.

Sexuality is a sensitive area for all adolescents, as they struggle to find new ways of relating to other people. The physical and emotional changes that take place at puberty mark the onset of this period. It is important that people working with learning disabled adolescents acknowledge their sexual feelings and impulses as being age-appropriate, yet do not deny the difficulties that can arise when there is a marked discrepancy between cognitive and physiological development.

An example would be that of John, a 13-year-old boy who is seen with his parents and siblings for psychoanalytic family therapy. John frequently touches his penis and clearly experiences exciting and disturbing genital sexual feelings, yet his favourite TV programmes and videos are those aimed at the under-5 audience, and he likes to play with brightly coloured toys designed for small children. He is severely brain-damaged and suffers from epilepsy.

John is a member of a loving family, and as a vulnerable young person, leads a protected life, whilst his parents encourage adolescent interests in every possible way. However, many of the learning disabled adolescents referred to us have been exposed to highly adverse circumstances. Their difficulties with regard to sexuality are, of course, exacerbated where there has been sexual abuse, and it may be part of the therapeutic task to help the young person learn to differentiate between a longing for closeness and affection appropriate to friendly and familial relationships, and their sexual desires which would ideally be expressed in intimate relationships.

I will now move on to some clinical material drawn from patients seen for individual psychotherapy. I will talk firstly about an 18-year-old young woman with a moderate learning disability and an eating disorder. I will then discuss a 16-year-old girl with Down's Syndrome, with a history of neglect, many changes of placement and sexual abuse, and conclude with some thoughts about a thirteen year old girl with a physical as well as a learning disability.

First Clinical Case: Elaine

Elaine is an 18-year-old young woman of Afro-Caribbean origin who had been assessed and for whom individual psychotherapy had been recommended. She lives with her mother who is a single parent.

I was very interested to work with Elaine to understand the nature of the link between her learning disability and her eating disorder – the two symptoms for which she had been referred by her mother. Non-learning disabled adolescents with eating disorders are quite often driven to prove themselves as being academic high-achievers, and I wondered if an equation between fatness and stupidity might be an aspect of the anxieties underlying anorexia, perhaps highlighted in this particular case.

Unfortunately, I was quickly to become acquainted with a difficult and painful issue that most learning disabled adolescents have to contend with, regarding attending the Clinic for therapy. It is that of their wish to be independent of parents or carers, in an age-appropriate way, offset against the problem of managing to travel to and from the Clinic alone.

For Elaine (who could travel by herself on public transport despite finding money difficult to manage) this was far less difficult than for most of our patients who have to be escorted, yet it still became a major stumbling-block which led to her having to be transferred to another therapist after only a few sessions with me.

39

First Therapy Sessions

An extract from Elaine's first therapy session follows:

Elaine arrived 10 minutes early. Her manner was friendly but guarded and anxious, and she was carefully dressed and made up. She spoke immediately of the problem of coming to the Clinic because she had to travel on the tube with little time to spare to fit in with her college timetable. She then talked of how tense she had been when she saw Mrs B for the assessment and how anxious she is everywhere; if she goes out she tenses up and hyperventilates and expects people to say things about her.

I talked about her coming to see me today; the difficulties of the journey, her worries about what I will say, and that despite these anxieties she has managed to come here. She spoke again of the problem of her timetable, and we worked out a change of time for therapy that might be more manageable. She said this was fine. I felt retrospectively that she had been over-accommodating.

She then talked about her two main problems; firstly, wanting to disappear, for nobody to see her, and secondly, being obsessed with dieting, a fear of being fat. She made a face when I said that her mum had phoned in advance of her session and mentioned this. I said that perhaps there is a connection between her two problems. I linked her wish to disappear with her wish to be thin, as if there is something about herself that she wants no one to know about. She talked of a fear of being fat, of seeing fat people in magazines and dreading that is how she will be seen. I talked to her of her possible worries about how she feels I will see her, and explained that this is something we can try to understand together. I added that she is perhaps feeling that I will have unkind thoughts in my mind.

She flushed and said that other children have always called her names, right through all her schools. She gave a long, painful account of this, beginning with nursery school, when a teacher told her to colour in the white bit of a picture and she couldn't. She then got behind with all her school work, seeing the other children able to do it, and they called her names. She felt so different from the other children. At her next school it was worse, so she stayed home and had a tutor for two years, which was very lonely.

I talked about a strong part of her who wanted to go back to school to be with other children. It is this part that has brought her here today. She wants to grow and develop – not to feel so badly about herself, and so afraid of what others are thinking about her, as if she feels that she is so different from them. She seems to feel that her learning problems are visible to all, and she wants to get rid of this part of herself.

She said she wants to go out and be a normal teenager. She is obsessed with dieting and can't eat lunch, even though she feels weak in the afternoons. She described her mum as overweight and always trying to make her eat more. We talked about her mixed feelings towards food, and perhaps towards therapy; of her knowing that there is something she needs, yet her fear that this is being forced upon her. This seemed to be connected with her anxiety about the time of the sessions; an expression of ambivalence.

We agreed to continue meeting but at a different time which she said she could manage. I felt very aware of a split transference – her perception of me as helpful and friendly on the outside, yet very different on the inside – critical and controlling. I had a sense that this corresponded to a harsh and judgmental internal object and that Elaine would blame herself for any lack of understanding in the therapeutic relationship. She conveyed a strong conviction that she felt there was something wrong with her, the nature of which suggested an equation of her learning disability with fatness, and a wish to get rid of this fat and stupid part of herself.

In the second session Elaine talked more of her anger and confusion. She described a fraught relationship with her mother which could flare up into rows, yet always ended up with Elaine blaming herself. She then told me proudly that she has begun to eat lunch, and decides what to have all by herself.

However, between the second and third sessions I received a number of phone calls from Elaine's mother telling me that Elaine cannot manage her sessions because the travelling is too difficult, and she misses too much time at college.

When I tried to discuss this with Elaine she was flustered and confused, and we agreed that I would explore the situation with her college tutor, and it may be possible to change her therapy time yet again.

Elaine did not appear for her fourth session and her mother phoned to tell me that she would not be coming again unless I could see her on a different day, one which was not possible for me.

I wrote to Elaine, and she replied in a letter that she did want to continue seeing me, but really could not manage travelling to and from her college. She came to one more session, where it was possible to face with her the conflicts involved in coming to the Clinic. Her old situation had been revived at college; she had to have extra help to make up for the time she lost in coming for her session, and this made her feel upset and confused; yet again, behind with her work and different from all the other students. She was ashamed to tell me this, and the session was painful but useful as we worked together in differentiating her anxieties from the reality of her situation.

She was relieved yet sad when we concluded that she would have to begin again with another therapist, in order to attend college and her therapy. However she did have an experience of clarifying her position and making her own decision.

Fortunately, a colleague could see Elaine immediately on a day when she did not have to negotiate college studies and difficult travelling, but I was left with the impression that Elaine felt that all this muddle and confusion had been her fault, rather than at least in part my failure to understand the implications of her learning disability in relation to her need for therapy.

This issue – of blaming herself – has arisen repeatedly in her therapy and can be usefully addressed. I was pleased to be able to supervise this case and hear of Elaine's continuing development. I would add that the apparent ease with which Elaine transferred from one therapist to another could also be understood in terms of her difficulty in identifying external factors as contributing to her problems; she only had complaints against herself. It is hard for her to shift to a symbolic mode and one in which difficulties are perceived by her as arising in relationships, not only within herself. She is making progress in gaining some distance from her learning disability and one may wonder if indeed the source of the disability lies in part in her internal object relationships rather than solely in herself.

Second Clinical Case: Beth

In therapeutic work with adolescent patients with Down's Syndrome I would like to suggest that the transference relationship arises in a particular way and has a different quality from that with which we are familiar in our work with other patients. Two 16 year olds with Down's Syndrome are currently in treatment, and there are interesting similarities in the quality of the transference relationship as perceived by the therapists. One of these two patients, Beth, whom I will describe below, has Down's Syndrome and a severe learning disability.

Firstly I will try to capture this quality to which I wish to draw attention. In the transference relationship between patient and therapist there is a sense of being in a dream-like state, and the therapist can feel rather as if she is participating in the patient's dream.

When the patient talks it is often not clear to whom he or she is referring – to him or herself or to the therapist – the direction is reversible. This mode of communication seems to lie somewhere between the concrete and the symbolic; there is meaning, but it is difficult to ascertain to what or to whom it can be attributed. It is as if there is a potential two-person relationship but the identities of subject and object are not clearly located. There is an 'I do this to you therefore you do this to me' quality to communications, again as in dreams.

From a different perspective, one could certainly say that these patients have a poor sense of self, or that there is very little ego development, but there seems to be a qualitative difference in the experience of being with this particular patient-group, that is both perplexing and fascinating. It is also rather exciting, as the way forward has to be discovered in the here-and-now of the session. It is as if one is working in uncharted territory, trying to locate which aspects of the patient's communications are familiar from one's usual therapeutic work, and which aspects are unfamiliar. Finding a way to understand the unfamiliar is challenging. It can also be daunting, and one can feel discouraged if the patient's material seems incomprehensible.

Sometimes it was difficult to comprehend Beth's communications as she related to her therapist in a way which was not familiar from clinical work with patients who are not learning disabled.

In Beth's first assessment session, she began with her head down and her eyes closed. There were four of us in the room; Jane (Beth's potential therapist), myself, Beth and a worker from her Children's Home. The difference between Beth aged 16 and with Down's Syndrome, and the three non-learning disabled adults felt acutely stark. She is very small for her age, plump and pale, with short straight hair unfashionably styled. She was dressed in a manner more suited to a young child than to an adolescent.

Beth kept her head down and her eyes closed whilst we spoke of the difficulty of the first visit to the Clinic. When I suggested that Beth might like to draw, she suddenly began to participate very actively in the session, drawing food and telling the three of us to do the same, handing out paper and pens. She drew our attention to ways in which we were the same; we all had black shoes, for example. This seemed to enable her to feel very much part of the session, instead of wanting to shut it out completely.

Beth's interest in all of us wearing black shoes seemed to me to be her way of saying 'we are all wearing black shoes so we are all the same'. I think this enabled her to participate, by obviating her unbearable sense of being so different.

One could of course interpret Beth's preoccupation with our all wearing the same coloured shoes as a defensive denial of painful differences. However, attempting to understand the character of her communication as being more in the realm of primary than secondary process can perhaps help the therapist to enter imaginatively into the state of mind of a person with Down's Syndrome.

Rather than being inclined to interpret the defensive manoeuvre, or perhaps Beth's wish that we were all the same, one can allow oneself to imagine her state of mind, the way in which at that point in time she perceives our shoes as all being the same colour, and then can feel that we are all the same.

I am grateful to Jane for Beth's material as individual therapy for Beth with Jane followed on from the assessment. I will give some background, then clinical material, to convey the quality of the sessions. The theme of sameness and difference reappears frequently.

Beth was referred to the Clinic by her care-workers at her Children's Home. There were several concerns about Beth's behaviour presented in this referral.

The staff were concerned that Beth was mimicking other residents' outbursts in order to vent her own anger. Beth was engaging in inappropriate sexual behaviour, e.g. touching young boys and male workers who live in the home and showing her body to strangers. The care-workers felt that Beth seemed ill at ease with herself and that her present living situation was adding to her confusion, frustration and anxiety.

When other residents had aggressive outbursts, sometimes of a psychotic nature, Beth herself would become aggressive and difficult to constrain. Her disruptive behaviour was paralleled by a disrupted continuity of relationships; there were frequent changes of residents and staff. However it also echoed her disrupted personal history. Beth was received into care at the age of one month; she was discharged back to her parents and siblings soon afterwards. The reason for this was not given, but one may speculate that it could have been her parents' ambivalence towards a baby with Down's Syndrome. During her early life, Beth was sent to live with an aunt in the North of England, but Social Services became involved when serious neglect was suspected, and at four years Beth was once more received into care. She lived with long-term foster carers, until the age of ten. This placement broke down following a lengthy investigation of suspected sexual abuse. Beth's teachers had been concerned about her sexual awareness and sexual acting out. It is not clear whether the allegations of abuse were substantiated. However, after the investigation, the family refused to see Beth.

She was temporarily removed to a Children's Home before being placed with new foster carers. Beth was said to have good relations with these parents; contact with her birth family had ceased and they were sensitive to her behavioural and emotional needs.

Some years later Beth's placement with this family broke down due to their ill health. She was moved to her current Children's Home, Elmhirst, in London where she has lived for the past year. Staff are concerned for Beth and, in addition to supporting her therapy, have requested consultation with regard to Beth's future placement.

First Therapy Session

Now follows an extract from Beth's first therapy session, which took place six weeks after the assessment and following a Christmas holiday. This is taken directly from Jane's material:

Beth and her care-worker arrived fifteen minutes late. I went to the reception area to meet her. When I arrived, she looked at me and then put her head down with her chin on her chest and closed her eyes. I said I wondered if she remembered me and asked if she wanted to come to the therapy room to talk. I explained that we would be going to a new room but that I still had her drawings from the last time she came to see me before Christmas ...

In the therapy room Beth immediately asked if I could move the table over so that she could draw. We moved the table. Beth asked to see her pictures.

I gave her the pictures and said I thought it had been difficult for Beth to start as it had been a long time since we met (six weeks) but that Beth remembered what she had done here before and she wanted to make sure I had kept the drawings.

Beth turned and put her hand on mine, she said my name, she asked me to shake her hand and greeted me again ... She took out the drawings from the assessment sessions. She picked one picture she had made of a bar of chocolate and said 'Elmhirst'. I asked if she was thinking about Elmhirst.

Beth started to colour the picture of the chocolate. She did not ask me to draw as she had done in the assessment sessions. Beth looked down at my legs. She noticed I was wearing black tights. She smiled and pointed to her legs, to show she was also wearing black tights. She said 'Same'. I said 'Yes – some things about us are the same'. Beth went on to compare my skirt, top and shoes with her own. She looked pleased that we both had black shoes on. Beth put her hand on mine and said, 'I like you' ... Beth looked at me and offered me her lipstick.

45

Commentary

Once in the therapy room, Beth re-establishes herself, remembering the drawings she had made in the assessment. Interestingly she comments first on her drawing of a bar of chocolate and says 'Elmhirst'. In the first assessment session in which I had been present Beth had drawn two rectangles, filled in with squares, and joined them together with a line. I had suggested to Beth that these two rectangles might be Elmhirst and the Tavistock Clinic and she is joining them together. She had turned to Jane and said 'It's chocolate' and I had felt foolish. I had wondered to myself how to understand this; a projection of stupidity as a means of Beth wanting me to know how she was feeling in the session? Or had I made a foolish interpretation, inappropriately symbolic for a learning disabled patient? I felt completely unsure at the time about this, but Beth's reference to this in her first therapy session with Jane suggests that she can internalise interpretations, which she may have perceived as meaningful.

For the third session Beth was again brought 15 minutes late by an agency escort. Jane felt that this escort infantilised and humiliated Beth, telling her to behave and be good, then she could have sweets. She was probably quite unaware of why Beth was coming to the Clinic and did not allow her the necessary time to respond to Jane in the waiting room. She told Beth off, threatening to tell her key worker at Elmhirst if she did not go with Jane right away. Beth refused to go with Jane until the escort had left the room to make a phone call – then she agreed immediately to go to the therapy room.

This again highlights a particular difficulty for many learning disabled adolescent patients. They are dependent upon an adult family member, carer or worker to organise and take them to their sessions. It happens quite frequently that the escort has not been given the opportunity to understand why the young person is being brought to the Clinic.

In this session Beth was withdrawn and impassive. After a while she did a drawing, filling a page with apples which she coloured brown. When Jane commented on Beth being fed up, she met Jane's eyes for the first time and looked very sad. Jane tried to talk with Beth about what might be preoccupying her and gained an impression from Beth's disparate responses, of words being linked together in a way which on the surface did not make sense, but if understood more as fragments in a dream, seemed to convey potential meaning. The words were like the apples on the page, randomly placed, yet with potential to form a narrative if they could be located in order, in time and space, in the therapist's mind.

At the end of this session, after Beth had left, Jane burst into tears. Beth's sadness had been received and contained by Jane, and, in the depth of this experience, understanding between them could begin to take shape.

It seems important not to underestimate Beth's intelligence, especially as in the fifth session there was a significant development in the therapy; an internal object relationship was enacted by Beth, giving a picture of a dirty, unwanted part of herself, which Beth wanted Jane to take care of, but also a harsh mocking part which tells Beth she is dirty. It was important to be vigilant for a projection into the therapist of this aspect of Beth, by which the therapist would find herself suddenly experienced as a persecutory object.

Fifth Therapy Session

Here is an extract from Jane's account of the fifth session. Note that a transformation occurs in the material at the point where Beth acknowledges difference. She perceives an asymmetrical relationship between herself and her therapist, which gives rise to persecutory anxiety. Jane is sensitive to this and Beth becomes able to convey verbally to Jane her feelings about being different from her therapist:

> ... Later in the session Beth offered me a crisp and again noticed our shoes were similar. She smiled and said, 'Shoes'. I said Beth often seemed pleased when she saw things were similar between us. I said some things are the same and some things are different. Beth asked me to choose a colour from the felt-tip pens. I chose red. She said 'No – wrong!' and chose blue. Beth then wrote on my hand; she said it was my name. Then she said 'Who are you, Jane?' I wondered if Beth was thinking about me and the ways we were different ...
>
> Beth then got up and said her escort's name. She went out of the door – I followed. I asked her if she wanted to know where her escort was. Beth followed me back down the stairs and towards the room. She then went into the next-door room. I tried to follow but she was leaning on the door, so that I could not get in. I said I thought Beth wanted to be away from me for a while and that I could wait in the room. Beth came out immediately and back to the therapy room. She sat down and continued to colour. She started to say 'Dirty cat – dog. Dirty pig'. She then got up and put her shirt in the toy box, saying 'Dirty'. I said I thought she might want to leave all the bad, dirty things here, with me. Beth said 'Yes' ...

47

Commentary

I would like now to raise the question of how best to understand the nature of Beth's communications. The dream-like quality of her sessions seems to indicate a potential for development, and to suggest that, as through interpretation of dreams, a more coherent narrative could emerge which links internal and external reality, and locates meaning in distinct individuals, who relate to each other in a non-reversible way. It remains an open question as to what extent an adolescent with a learning disability like Down's Syndrome can develop cognitively and emotionally through the therapeutic process. Jane's work with Beth suggests that quite quickly, object relationships can be clarified and the patient can develop a capacity for self/object differentiation that facilitates emotional and cognitive development. The transference can be interpreted if one bears in mind that the session may be characterised by primary process 'thinking' as in dreams, and that the identities of patient and therapist may be fluid and reversible in the patient's mind. Development in the therapeutic relationship takes place at points where self and object can be clearly differentiated and experienced as having distinct identities.

Third Clinical Case: Jennifer

This last brief extract is from my work with a younger disabled adolescent; a 13-year-old girl. Jennifer has had a physical disability from birth – a serious spine deformation – as well as a moderate learning disability. I have chosen this piece of clinical material because I think it highlights the painful situation which adolescents with disabilities have to confront. They long to be like other teenagers, beginning a period of life in which there is less parental control, with a very strong pull towards identifying with a peer group.

Teenagers notoriously want all to be the same; same clothes, same music and so on. Disabled adolescents invariably feel they are different in a profound way. This is often the case even when there is a mild learning disability which is not visible. This sense of difference is usually experienced in terms of feeling of lower value than others, and sometimes of being inherently bad and rejected as such.

Of course these feelings can be socially reinforced as there is a strong tendency in society for disabled people to be looked down upon and treated as inferior. From an internal perspective, one can speculate that the intensity and pervasiveness of such feelings suggests that they originate in early infancy; perhaps in the parents' disappointment in having given birth to a disabled baby, which no matter how much the parents try not to communicate this to their child, may play a part in the very low self-esteem characteristic of people with disabilities.

For the disabled adolescent, the desire to be part of a non-disabled adolescent group with whom to identify can be very powerful. However, mitigating against this desire is a conviction that other adolescents will treat them in a cruel way. From a social perspective, this can be generated by the experience of being bullied and mocked, but a contributing internal factor can be that of jealousy on the part of the disabled adolescent of non-disabled peers, and jealousy in itself can contribute to the sense of being irrevocably different.

Jennifer, aged thirteen years, was referred through her GP by her parents because they felt that she had become acutely unhappy with the onset of puberty. Although she attends a school for 'delicate' children with a variety of special needs, she is the only one with a very obvious physical deformation, although a small number of other children, like Jennifer, are wheelchair bound. She is highly sensitive to this, and attributes her difficulties in sustaining friendships to the visible nature of her disability which she feels highlights her difference from her peers. She is a pretty, rather fragile-looking girl who likes to wear fashionable clothes. Despite her strongly stated negative feelings about her appearance with regard to her disability, she is clearly proud of her long, silky blonde hair.

Third Session

Jennifer was waiting for me in the entrance hall in a different wheelchair from usual. This one was very large, cumbersome and not electric. She smiled at me without meeting my eyes and asked me to push her. Once in the therapy room she immediately talked about her problems, centred firstly upon her non-disabled older sister who can do all the things Jennifer would like to do, and then upon other girls at her school who she said would sometimes be friendly to her and sometimes bully her, in what she experienced as an arbitrary manner. She talked of trying to get away from them in her wheelchair but they would follow her.

I commented on her current wheelchair, this being one where she cannot get away; she cannot go anywhere by herself but has to ask to be pushed, and I think this must be very hard for her. It must make her feel very vulnerable to all these other children, who may or may not be friendly. She said her electric wheelchair is part of her but it is broken. 'It will be fixed Friday, so it doesn't matter.' She quickly went on to talk at length about a plan that she knew about to make all schools begin at 8 a.m. so she will be very tired at having to get up at 5 a.m. to catch the school bus. She said that the teachers do not know about this yet, nor does her mum, but they will be very tired. It does not make sense.

I wondered if she was telling me how very tiring it is for her to get around. She tells me that there is a plan to make life difficult for everyone that she knows about, and nobody else knows this. I said that I thought she feels life is so hard when you feel pushed around, you don't always know what is going to happen next, and you have limited choice because you are in a wheelchair. I said I thought she must mind very much about not having her own electric wheelchair which does give her more choice.

She smiled and said yes, she did, but there was not anything she could do about it. She was born like this. She once tried to walk but she couldn't. I said I thought she would like me to know how much she would like to be more in control of her life, to be able to make plans and carry them out herself. She does get very frustrated.

Jennifer said in response to this: 'I had a dream last night; a nightmare. I fired the school over and over again, and it came down on top of me'. We talked about how frustrating it is for her to be so full of angry feelings but not being able to do anything about this. The anger goes on and on inside her until she feels that everything gets on top of her, too much to manage. Jennifer said that in the dream the teachers were laughing. They were laughing and smoking and taking drugs.

I knew that Jennifer was sensitive to the transference implications of this and could easily feel that I would in my mind be laughing in a callous way at her predicament. I felt that so early on in my work with her, bearing in mind her learning disability, she may hear an interpretation of this kind as a confirmation. I instead talked about how she makes the teachers in her dream sound like teenagers having a good time. This is something which is on her mind; how can she be a teenager and do the things that teenagers do when they have not got disabilities? She agreed in a downcast voice and I asked her if anything else happened in the dream?

She said that someone pulled her out and then went straight on to talk rather unclearly about a friend who gave her a bracelet. She smiled as she showed me a thin blue plastic band on her arm of a kind that were popular with teenage girls at that time. I thought to myself about her wish for me to pull her out of the crushing restrictions of her disability

50

and help her into the world of adolescence. Again, it seemed unwise to interpret in this way as it may have conveyed the impression that I had a magical capacity actually to do this. (The painful nature of this kind of work is more concerned with helping young people to be able to bear the limitations of their disabilities yet not retreat from relationships with others.)

I asked Jennifer about the girl who gave her the bracelet and she said that she was her friend but she also bullied Jennifer. She emphasised that this girl was fourteen and had a behaviour disorder, not a disability.

I wondered about the mixed qualities attributed to the teachers in the dream, as if the laughing, smoking, drug-taking teachers were the non-disabled adolescents who behave in a disordered but exciting way and who provoke jealousy and frustration in Jennifer. Yet they are also perceived as engaging in dangerous and unhealthy pursuits (Jennifer said to me that she would never smoke or take drugs), and as a mocking, bullying gang who jeer at her disability.

It seemed safe to say to Jennifer that she did get pulled out in her dream, and she does hope that I will be able to help her with these very difficult feelings about becoming a young woman and wanting to join in with teenage life.

In conclusion, I hope I have conveyed the point that the issue of sameness and difference is salient in therapeutic work with adolescents with disabilities. The more severe the disability, perhaps the more acute is the preoccupation with being different, but it seems to be a very painful dilemma for many disabled young people when they reach the age at which it is so important to be part of the peer group.

Acknowledgement

I am grateful to my colleague Nancy Sheppard for sharing with me her expertise in working with patients with Down's Syndrome.

Confrontation, Appeasement or Communication?

Jonathan Bradley

It is to be expected that therapeutic work with adolescents will take on some of the characteristics of adolescence itself. This, however quiet on the outside (though it frequently is not quiet!), is marked by inner turmoil. Much of the turmoil concerns the renegotiating of positions with regard to authority figures. Even though they may not wish to be so, parents, with their weight, presence and sense of achievement are seen as formidable. Communication is difficult within such 'uneven' relationships. Instead there is direct confrontation or an appeasement of authority which can hide an angry resentment.

A powerful example of the way in which the adolescent's search for a unique identity can in fact be a turning away from what has already been achieved by earlier generations, was given by Richard Olivier. In the television programme 'From Here to Paternity' (one of a series of Men-Only Documentaries) he spoke powerfully of the difficulty in following in father's footsteps. As a teenager he set out to be as different from his father as possible: 'Where he relied on instinct, I tried to base my actions on thoughts. While he was an actor I was determined to become a writer and director'. Chillingly, his father's death gave him a sense of elation, as he realised that 'the stage' was now clear. This sense of triumph is perhaps hard to understand when one thinks of Lord Olivier and all that he achieved. It is more understandable, when seen in terms of a son desperately trying to find a bit of the world for himself that had not been conquered by his colossus of a father. It proved to be a short lived triumph as he tried to mourn the person whom he felt he really had not known properly as a father, but only as a public actor. He was nevertheless able to enter into a process of mourning, during which a memory came to him of when he was five. He remembered looking up at his father 'blacked up' to play Othello. He was like a King.

When he recalled this scene from his childhood he was able to see it in a different way. He realised that what he had taken for aloofness and coldness was in fact an extraordinary courage against the enemy of cancer to which his father had fallen prey. Communication with his father properly took place after Lord Olivier's death. Part of this process was to dismantle the view of his father which was built up around the issue of dominance against which he campaigned as an adolescent. In its place there developed a perspective which could admire and respect Lord Olivier for what he had done and yet disagree with what he called the 'stiff upper lip tradition'. He determined that his son, Troy, would not experience the same degree of isolation that he himself had suffered: 'I try to spend as much time as I can with him, to let him be involved with me and my life – whether I am writing in my office or cooking eggs'.

The story of confrontation and eventual reconciliation through a process of communication is common enough though given added weight by the fame of the participants. A key element in Richard Olivier's sense of alienation was the feeling that only by rejecting his father's values completely could he hope to find a place for himself. Underlying the determination to challenge father's values one by one, lay a rather desperate need to be recognised in his own right, though it seems that this could not be asked for directly.

Before giving clinical examples I would like to return briefly to the theme of adolescence. Teenagers particularly between the ages of sixteen and eighteen, are searching for a new identity but on the way encounter a lot of confusion and contradictions within themselves. A child and a more grown-up self co-exist and alternate in unexpected and unpredictable ways. The complaint of many parents of this age group is that like any child they may be impulsive, omnipotent and demanding of instant gratification, but they also have a capacity for strong passionate emotions and surprising devotion and concern for good causes. There is also a growing intellectual capacity to question received ideas whilst developing their own. Teenagers are beset with uncertainties: Who are they? What will they become? What is their place in the world? Anxieties such as these are not confined neatly to one particular area such as family life. Instead, the same kind of issues embracing radical reorganisation involves school life, leading often to enormous disillusionment with school generally and the process of learning, friendship and social life. It involves painful and very public re-evaluation of friendships, and often, the forming of groups and gangs. Perhaps the most massive re-appraisal is taking place within the body itself where

54

sexual development, including masturbation, falling in love, the embracing of a changed sexual identity, break up and break down in relationships, the need for contraception, a time of pregnancy, even abortion, frequent changes of sexual partners all seem to occur with bewildering frequency, often within the same person.

This is, then, a time when all who work with teenagers in many different areas, including parents and teachers and counsellors, are often bewildered by the rapidity of change. It can seem that the person who you thought you knew the day before appears the next day in an entirely different frame of mind, a different personality. It is a time when the impact on people outside is merely a reflection of the bewildering change of scene that is happening within. For the teenager too, seems to be very bewildered by the rapidity of change. This is the time when there are frantic attempts to bind teenagers to contracts, to get them to sign on the dotted line, to appear regularly at classes, to appear regularly at counselling sessions, to take due responsibility for cleaning their room. The frustration of adults, when the next day after making a contract with a teenager they find themselves confronted with the same body with no apparent recollection of having signed anything and certainly no sense of responsibility to carry it through, is perhaps matched by the puzzlement that the teenager may also face that a stranger, admittedly in his own body, could have agreed to something which today he feels does not remotely answer his needs! Understandably such inconsistency can be met quite reprovingly both by adults and by a self-critical part of teenagers themselves. 'Lack of discipline', 'lack of consistency', 'uncaring' tend to be by-words that crop up with a lot of frequency. Whilst of course, these qualities or weaknesses of character may well indeed be part of the picture, the deeper reason for the great pace of shift of attitude is to be found in the massive change from child-like feelings to more adult feelings that can come upon an adolescent quickly.

It is of little surprise to find that every attempt to work consistently with adolescents, particularly those who are inclined to be involved in active exploration of their identity, will lead to the same turbulence being brought into the psychotherapeutic setting.

First Clinical Example: Emma

Emma was a fifteen-year-old girl who had been referred to a Counselling Service following a serious overdose of Paracetamol. After taking the tablets she had told a friend what she had done and the Emergency

Services had been notified. Emma was reported to have said that she would never speak again to the friend who had betrayed her confidence, cheating her of death. There was every indication that Emma might well make another attempt on her life.

I do remember going into the meeting in a very alert frame of mind, very much aware of the need to try to hold on to someone who I thought might be volatile. She started by telling me that she had a friend, Rachel, who is in regular therapy. Her friend could say anything to her therapist and she felt that it would be good for Emma to do so. I was taken by surprise by this start and did, however, keep at the back of my mind the friend who had been rejected though saving her life. I explained that she seemed to want to talk about herself. Perhaps she could tell me what she particularly wanted to think about? She said that before doing so she wanted to lay down certain conditions. I found myself thinking 'here comes the friend'. I needed to know that she was a confirmed lesbian and that she had no intention of discussing that decision and she wanted me to make a commitment to avoid that topic during our discussions. If I couldn't promise that, then she would have to leave. After this beginning I did find it difficult to think, but what I did know was, at that moment, it would not be useful to get into a discussion about lesbianism.

What I ended up saying was 'Rachel had given her a picture of what therapy was about, Rachel seemed to be able to go in and say anything at all and keep nothing to herself, but maybe it was not that easy. She had just met me, how did she know what my own prejudices were? How could she begin to trust me? I understood her to be saying that she would be keeping some things to herself and I would respect this and not ask her to tell me about things that she did not want to talk about'. She said that it was important because some people felt that she had tried to kill herself because she was unhappy at school and was being bullied. In fact she had tried to kill herself because she had lost the best girlfriend she had ever had. Her parents had taken her back to Asia because they felt she was a bad influence on her. They felt that she had corrupted her. This made her feel very bad and also, since they were involved in an ongoing lesbian relationship, it made her feel that she had lost a part of herself and could not be bothered to keep herself alive. I felt that it was important to continue her line of thought, but I was also concerned that she was in fact talking about lesbianism and she had wanted me not to talk about it. I said that it did seem as if she did want to talk about her own views on lesbianism and perhaps feel that I would be able to listen to these. I said that I was very struck by her thought

56

that what was left in her after her friend was taken away was the bit of her that was like rubbish that she did not want, and therefore, killing it would be killing something worthless. She then said 'Everyone else seems to think it is anyway, so why should I think any different?'

During the session she spoke in a very moving way and I felt that after a very volatile start to the meeting I was now more in the presence of somebody who was telling me about a neglected childhood, of not being taken seriously, something that I could empathise with. I asked her to tell me why she thought that. She then went on to explain that she would not be in this mess if it had not been for her father who left her and her mother in a way that caused a major scandal. He gambled heavily and went off to a part of the world where they discovered he had another family. She described, with very great anguish, the trauma for herself and her mother to discover what he had done and the complications for them. At face value, she said, he had seemed a good father. I said that what had struck me more than anything about her story was the feeling of deception: that you could not tell on the outside what was happening underneath. Had she felt on coming to the room here, that whilst I might on the surface be seeming to listen to her, underneath I would be scheming.

This did not seem to be what she wanted to hear and ignoring it seemingly, she said that since her father left, when she was ten, she has placed more trust in friends of her own age than in adults. I felt there was a trap opening up and I decided not to say anything. After a while she said 'I suppose you are thinking that's why I became a lesbian'. I said she had not actually told me why she had become a lesbian only that she was confirmed in her choice and did not want me to query it. I had also said that I would be pleased to think with her about her thoughts and perhaps she was not sure about that, maybe she did feel I was coming with my own agenda, simply wanting to turn her to my way of thinking. This did seem to be more satisfactory from her point of view and she went on to other issues and indeed over the next few months has continued to bring a bewildering variety of parts of herself. I cannot go into detail here, but it might be of interest to know that the very next week the first topic she raised was that of contraception and whether parents needed to know about 15-year-olds that had sex.

Before considering the other example, I will mention one aspect of the process of thought that I found myself in. Undoubtedly I did go in with the hope that I would manage to engage this girl in an ongoing relationship so that there would be adequate time to look at some of the bewildering changes of states of mind. I don't know what bottom line I had, what I would have been prepared to do to keep her, but it did seem that part of the process of communication, that is communication about the reason why she was prepared to take her own life, did involve making a decision not to pursue other topics which were presented as diversions to this main task.

Second Clinical Example: Jabed

I want now to turn to Jabed who was an adolescent seen in the context of a school for emotionally and behaviourally disturbed children. He was in fact seen over a period of a number of years, he was 14 when the particular incident I shall report took place. Up to that point he had had a very difficult life. He had been born prematurely by Caesarean section with congenital impaired hearing and had very poor eyesight. He had known many painful separations in life, the first at three years when mother left father. Temporary care situations followed until she took Jabed and his brother David, one year younger, to live with her and a new partner. Jabed developed an asthmatic condition and persistent bedwetting when he was 4-and-a-half for which he was referred for psychotherapy to a Child Guidance Unit. This stopped after a term when the therapist became ill. Soon after this Jabed's behaviour, at school and home, deteriorated. He was controlled by harsh treatment and both children were admitted to hospital several times. On one occasion Jabed had wounds to his head and cigarette burns on his hand. Father came back on the scene and successfully got custody of the children. He had been in the army and applied what he regarded as needed discipline. There was no suggestion that he hit the children, but he controlled them very firmly. He could not understand how Jabed, in particular, was regarded as so spiteful and aggressive at school since he was so meek at home. It was his school record that led to his being referred to a special school and since then the meek part of Jabed had developed into a deeply passive Jabed and on occasions a masochistic Jabed who would engineer situations in which he could be punished and when this failed, would hit himself. On the other hand there was the aggressive, spoiler, deeply abusive, using language according to one report 'of a quality not used by the other children and this in an EBD school'. There seemed little contact between the two sides of his personality, neither side was trusted.

At first when he saw me he did seem to make good progress, his behaviour improving quite remarkably within the school. However, as he grew further into adolescence it seemed as if he brought more and

58

more into the therapy situation, the unsuccessful results of his attempt to renegotiate with a rather stern father on matters of discipline and responsibility. With some justification he felt that father treated him like a little child. This made him angry and all the more irresponsible. At the time I am writing about he had become more and more volatile at the day school, setting fires, and at home, on one occasion, turning the gas on before going out. It seemed as if he was making an *explosive* bid to destroy the home and destroy the possibility of remaining at the day school where he lit the fires, which, had they occurred at home, would indeed have led to an explosion.

Within the therapy situation I was becoming convinced that we would have to stop seeing each other. More and more Jabed had lost the ability to express things imaginatively. Increasingly it seemed that there was no buffer between us, nothing to stop us clashing verbally but also physically. Our world was one where he would make a furious rushing entry into the room taking it over trying to dominate it and me. He would push into me as I sat, attempt to sit on me, attempt to get inside, or stand on the arm of the chair straddling me. He would even dare me to speak on pain of being 'peed' on as punishment and yet at the same time it became obvious from what he said that he needed me to speak. There was indeed a child expressing his need for dependency, listening to me intently and being moved as I spoke. There was also a gloating adolescent glorying in power and confusing this with a push to independence. He would tell me that since I had spoken so I would have to be punished by being 'peed' on.

Though I managed to stop this happening, the dilemma was always the same: how to refuse to be drawn into these sexualised games of power and submission whilst keeping open dialogue? When a 'word' did speak to Jabed it was impossible to know what its effect would be. Sometimes the thought would be allowed to remain but usually the intensity of the claustrophobic presence would be ousted as it were, by a rush to explode outwards into a space that knew no bounds and certainly not the confining space of the therapy room.

This rapid oscillation between a conflict in claustrophobic space and an explosion into fragmented space can be used appropriately to describe many therapy situations, whether they be children, adolescents or adults, where the essential issue is the avoidance of pain. But there is a difference in quality where the conflict is immediately externalised into physical violence, because no fantasy is available. There is a difference in quality too between the violence of a young child and that of an adolescent. Such violence is not tolerated for long and it is hard

59

to think that it should be. I am mentioning the case of Jabed here however, because there was a stroke of luck.

Perhaps something of my desperate search for some way of lessening the immediacy of contact between us communicated itself to Jabed. On his return from one of his, by now regular periods of suspension from school for starting a fire in the school playground, he somehow managed not to simply burst in but announced instead that he would sit in the lobby area just outside the therapy room. As you came from the corridor outside you found yourself in a little lobby, there was another door to be gone through that, when closed, would made an enclosed room attached to the larger therapy room. Until then, frankly, it had been a nuisance posing many boundary issues, but now given some good will on Jabed's part it was what made it possible to continue with therapy at a crucial time. There followed much negotiation over its specific use during sessions, but in essence I allowed him to sit in it, but the inner door had to be kept open, keeping some communication. Some days this was as little as an inch carefully measured out! I found myself musing quite a lot about the function of this little room attached to the bigger room. I felt that at one level it was a prison cell where he would end up accused of violent crime if he were not to gain some control over his impulses, but it became a place where gradually what might be called an intrapsychic buffer came to operate, something that could be interposed between impulse and action.

From the vantage point of this room it became possible for Jabed to start to visualise the probable results should a dimly perceived fantasy for violence be concretised into an aggressive deed. For the first time it was possible to talk about what might happen if he did something rather than always having to deal with the consequences of his actually having done something. To some extent his thinking seemed to do with realising that if he did not do something he would end up in a cell like this. But as well as standing for a prison cell the room came to mean something much more positive. I think it helped an infantile part of him to catch up with the flow of action in the sessions. The door made it possible for him to control the flow of my words, to take his time about responding and not to worry about being in silence which was far less threatening now he could not see me. In this way he was showing his great fear of being overwhelmed by what he experienced as a very powerful presence that he could not control. The door gave him control. It had the sense of a very primitive process like a baby finding that he can control the flow of milk and avoid being flooded and choked by the mother's breast. I also feel that the Spartan surroundings of the lobby with its wooden bench and walls that he could touch easily placed him in contact with a 'no frills' (rather than a 'no thrills') mother that he could cope with, one who knew how to hold on the lap without giving a cuddle until she felt it was needed. It turned out that the introduction of this way of using the therapy space led to a significant development in the kind of topics that could be discussed. I mention it because I feel that it is a useful image of what I mean by the process of establishing communication, particularly where volatile adolescents are concerned.

During my time with Jabed I came to think about what happened in the lobby, as 'the room for some thought' and feel that it can be seen as an analogy. The first thing to be said about it is that it occupied a relatively small proportion of the overall space and yet it had an effect far larger than its size would have led one to think. It was also in some ways an artificial creation: it had to be kept in place by continued fussy involvement in issues such as opening the door, and action over constant attempts to take over the space to use it for other purposes. The result was to make emotional nutrition possible. I was able to be more receptive by allowing myself to have more thoughts without having to defend my right to have it. It seemed that I was only able to let Jabed grow inside me once I put distance between us at an external level. I think it was possible to be far more sensitive and delicate as a result. Within the therapy situation, with adolescents there will be a similar need to create some internal space where one can be left alone. Tolerating the situation runs counter to an understandable, though impulsive, wish to have a fight and have it all over with! If one can be in control of these processes then the result can be a gradual focusing on the main issue and an opening up of the therapeutic involvement, through an atmosphere of communication.

Discussion

In the examples given, 'communication', when it arrived, was unexpected and dramatic. Richard Olivier, in mourning, was confronted by the huge figure of Othello. The realisation that what he had mistaken for aloofness was in fact a courageous stance against the enemy of cancer followed on from this dramatic memory. This communication, a glimpse of a father he had misunderstood made it possible for him to subject himself to self-scrutiny and helped him to challenge a hostile view of his father. Over time he managed to move away from a system based on being the absolute opposite to his father. Clearly, building a

61

personality and career from this basis would be impoverishing on two counts. Firstly it would mean that father's positive attributes were denied him since he had pledged to seek out their opposite. Secondly, such a stance would involve turning a deaf ear to his own thoughts and feelings about the kind of person he would like to become. The eventual outcome, the development of a system of values influenced by, but being able to be independent of, father's values, was brought about, one would think, by a process of change that involved the painful reorganisation of familiar values. Inevitably then, change is instinctively resisted if for no other reason that it raises the prospect of a life without familiar values and relationships.

The demands on a therapist working in such a situation are particularly demanding. Wilfred Bion stressed that in such situations it is important for us as therapists to look for ways of helping a client become familiar with a particular aspect of truth about the situation. He contrasts this with two other possible positions: the telling of various forms of agreeable lies which I have thought of as 'appeasement' in this chapter; or confronting the client with an insight in such a frightening form that emotional paralysis results. In the examples given, of Emma and Jabed, it seemed very important to be actively searching for a way through by formulating questions such as: is it useful to discuss the issue of lesbianism with Emma at this point, or is the topic being brought in to defend against other anxieties such as the feeling of abandonment by father and the subsequent loss of trust in adults? In the example of Jabed, the situation was so fraught that words, particularly where there was visual contact, had become impossible. In this unusual situation the fact that there was still the possibility of communication had literally to be measured out in inches by means of the ruler. This 'rule' insisted that there be some opening between his place and mine at all times.

As far as we therapists are concerned there is a difficulty that compromise, and the adapting of a therapeutic technique can become an 'agreeable lie' where nothing 'muscular' can be said and where the primary purpose of therapy (the possibility of emotional insight) becomes lost. How to avoid this? In such situations, particularly with teenagers, it seems important to be able to draw an analogy from the common experience of families where there are teenagers. Here the pressure to relax boundaries can be enormous, as can be the temptation to impose inflexible arrangements more suitable for a young child rather than a teenager. At times a situation seems to develop where there is both a strong push for independence and at the same time reassuring dependence. Parents are commonly placed in a situation of

62

feeling oppressive if they impose rules, and uncaring if they don't. It seems important to continue to set boundaries and yet maintain a dialogue about them which allows appraisal.

What does this entail? To continue the analogy: it is useful for parents to be in touch with their own adolescence and its turbulence, when trying to maintain dialogue with a teenager! As far as therapy is concerned, therefore, it seems particularly important that therapist and client are not felt to inhabit 'different planets'. Dina Rosenbluth, a child analyst, when looking at the question of what is entailed by the achieving of 'insight' in therapy, develops the concept of 'knowledge by acquaintance', as opposed to that of 'knowledge by description'.

It is possible to build up a picture of something by accumulating facts, but in such a way that the enquirer remains untouched by the process. 'Knowledge by acquaintance', on the other hand, implies that a process of discovery is shared. Communication, when it takes place, arises from the realisation that the therapist is willing to make a journey similar to that of the client.

References

Bick, E. (1968) 'The experience of the skin in early object relations', *International Journal of Psychotherapy*, 49: 484.

Hoxter, S. (1964) 'The experience of puberty', *Journal of Child Psychotherapy*.

Meltzer, D. (1992) *The Claustrum, An Investigation of Claustrophobic Phenomena*, Roland Harris Trust Library 15, Clunie.

Symington, J.S. (1996) *The Clinical Thinking of Wilfred Bion*, London: Routledge.

Rosenbluth, D. (1968) '"Insight" as an aim of treatment', *Journal of Child Psychotherapy*, 2, 2: p. 5.

Williams, A. (1982) 'Adolescents, violence and crime', *Journal of Adolescence*, 5: p. 125.

Williams, M.H. (1987) *Collected Papers of Martha Harris and Esther Bick*, Clunie (1987), section IV, pt. 5, p. 340, Bion's conception of a psycho-analytical attitude.

Further Reading

Bradley, J. and Dubinsky, H. (1994) *Understanding 15-17 Year Olds*, Rosendale Press.

5

Suicidal Behaviour and Its Meaning in Adolescence

Robin Anderson

Introduction

In this chapter I intend to approach the issue of adolescent suicide and attempted suicide from the point of view of what is going on in the minds of young people who deliberately harm themselves and then to consider some of the problems we encounter when we try to help them.

I think it is relevant to set the scene against which these private or sometimes public tragedies are set. Suicides by men outnumber those by women by a ratio of more than 2:1. In adolescents, this rate is even higher at 3:1. Moreover, the suicide rates amongst young men in the UK and Europe from 15 to 24 have increased by 75% since the mid nineteen eighties. Adolescent suicide constitutes the largest cause of death after accidents for this age group. Amongst adolescents who attempt suicide by overdoses, (studies vary) up to 50% will repeat the act within twelve months and somewhere between 1 and 11% will eventually kill themselves. The picture obtained from these large studies shows that amongst young men, significant factors are drug and alcohol problems, social isolation, poor economic conditions, the presence of bullying, a history of physical and sexual abuse and being held in custody. Women tend to make more attempts at suicide, while men are more successful in the attempts that they do make probably because men choose more physically destructive methods e.g. hanging and shooting. Amongst women, additional factors are poor socialisation and sense of identity, a high degree of family problems especially with fathers and an over-representation in Asian young women. Of course, behind these rather anonymous statistics lies personal tragedy and inner dramas which I will try to throw some light on in this chapter. For a more detailed account of the epidemiology of suicide see Shaffer and Piacentini (1994) and Brent D.A. (1997).

When we look at why an individual will make an attempt on his own life, we are dealing with the culmination of a whole series of complex forces which beset the individual and we cannot always know what these are. The problem with this subject is that both in studying it and working with individuals who harm themselves, we are confronted by primitive processes and fears which can in turn stir up our own anxieties which can then lead us to try to distance ourselves from the problem.

In Europe during most of the Christian era, suicide was regarded with even greater condemnation, and therefore presumably fear, than murder. The unsuccessful suicide was not only punished severely, but the successful suicides could not be buried in an ordinary cemetery. They had to be buried at a cross-roads either with a stake through the heart or with stones on top of the body to prevent their spirit rising and haunting the living. Shakespeare refers to this in A Midsummer Night's Dream where Puck says:

> 'And yonder shines Aurora's harbinger,
> At whose approach ghosts, wand'ring here and there,
> Troop home to churchyards. Damned spirit all,
> That in cross-ways and floods have burial,
> Already to their wormy beds are gone,
> For fear lest day should look their shame upon;
> They wilfully themselves exil'd from light,
> And must for aye consort with black-brow'd night.'
> (William Shakespeare, *A Midsummer Night's Dream*,
> Act Three, Scene II, Lines 380-7.)

Here Shakespeare refers to the burial of murderers and suicides at crossroads and the 'floods' in which people had drowned themselves and are left permanently excluded from society even after their deaths. The fear seemed to be that such a terrible act would come back and infect the living. Although we have now done away with these barbaric and superstitious practices, suicide was illegal until 1961 and it was still possible to be sent to prison for attempted suicide. This seems to reflect the primitive fear which is still with us when we face what humans can do to themselves, and the emotional forces that motivate them Alvarez (1971). Interestingly there are many studies which suggest that especially amongst adolescents there is strong evidence to show that suicide is 'contagious' – for example when the suicide of prominent individuals results in a spate of copy suicides which follow the media reports (see Gould and Shaffer, 1986). There are also well observed clusters or epidemics of suicide in certain groups such as the children at a school (see Gould, 1990). Many professionals who assess suicides in accident and emergency departments have observed institutional defences against the proper management of attempted suicides as though reflecting a modern day equivalent of historical attitudes and some departments can be very harsh to those who harm themselves. The attempted suicide can be treated with contempt and sometimes outright cruelty which goes far beyond the understandable irritation of busy staff dealing with someone who is responsible for their own condition.

Two Examples: Sanjay and Anne

Sanjay, a young man of seventeen, was referred to our department having taken a serious overdose of paracetamol. He had a history of very long-standing, rather bizarre treatment by a very disturbed father. He had been kept in a cot until he was nine and after that, forced to sleep with his father though apparently, was not explicitly sexually abused, and until fifteen he was washed by his father. He was full of hatred for him and wanted to kill him, and indeed, tried to poison him using mercury from a thermometer and when that failed with hay fever pills. When that failed too, he did not escalate his attacks on his father but instead he made several suicide attempts which resulted in his reception into care.

This was, of course, a particularly strange form of upbringing, but even though at the point of referral we had very little information on him, it was still possible to draw some conclusions about his behaviour. It was clear that he wanted to free himself from his father's mad hold over him, but this seemed to include the idea that the only escape was by death. When his attempt on his father's life failed (and it probably failed because his attempts were very half-hearted) – and when his wish to free himself increased, instead of becoming more violent towards his father, he then tried to break free by removing himself from the situation by his own death. This suggested that he now felt it would be better to kill himself than to kill his father and that he not only hated his father but also loved him, and he found it less painful to kill himself. Fortunately his attempt was heard as a cry for help, whether or not it was intended as such, and he was taken into care by social services, still troubled but with the risk of death having lessened.

Anne, a young woman of 16, was referred to us following multiple suicide attempts. These ranged from using lighter fuel and making herself unconscious, to overdoses, to cutting herself. These attempts were of varying severity – some seemed merely gestures while others, really put her life in danger requiring treatment in intensive care units. When any level of anxiety seemed to be mobilised in her, she would become agitated and want to run away to seek oblivion, either partially with drugs or gas, or to cross the line towards clear suicide attempts. She was an 'anonymous' girl, no-one knew her real name or had contact with her family and she was taken on as the responsibility of social services. Her social worker found her a tremendous burden, almost a full time job.

Anne said she had run away from a family in which she had been sexually abused by her father who had threatened to kill himself if it ever came out. Anne was also sabotaging every kind of help she was offered and at this time, had been through our care, three or four social services homes, an adolescent unit and several foster placements. She seemed to find good experiences as disturbing as bad ones, for example she was placed for a time with a foster mother who she said she really liked but still ran away suggesting that for her to be having loving feelings towards helpful figures stirred up emotions that she could not stand.

In this way, she seemed to communicate a sense of desperation in those who were trying to help her and a sense that there was no place that she could be, no place where she could find peace and rest, and running through it with crescendos and diminuendos was a sense that the only emotional space she could inhabit was one where she was constantly on the edge of death. It was as though she could neither bring herself to really ask for help to reclaim her family, because this would entail betraying her father which she believed would result in his death, but nor could she commit suicide. The only alternative was to live on the edge of both, life and death and this was like a claustrophobia which threatened unbearable persecution from which she had to escape. It was as though her loving feelings about her family and her sense of needing to be cared for were so mixed up with her hatred, her sense that this was a terrible place where terrible things had been done to her were quite mixed up with her sense that this was *her* family and included even her father, and this confusion was experienced with anyone else who behaved in a parental way towards her. She did not know whether to love or hate, to stay or go.

Thus, unlike Sanjay, Anne could not seek help straightforwardly. As soon as she found something good that might put her in touch with the family that she had lost, she became persecuted and had to escape though escape was usually to a false haven. Often it was a group of friends who would share her wish for oblivion and they would sniff gas together, as she had done with her brother, as though this group of young people in trouble like herself were turned to in preference to the adult world which had let her down so badly. What particularly struck me about Anne was that unlike so many young people in London, she really had been offered good help; she had not been treated with disdain by the hospital which admitted her unconscious from the local train station, she had been assigned a social worker who had worked tirelessly with her, she had been offered a whole range of help but somehow, all this seemed either to make no difference or to make her worse. This contrasted so markedly with the state of Sanjay who was able to move to a foster home and study for his A levels, troubled, angry and confused, but able to grasp and use what had been offered to him.

It is often very striking to consider the differences between young people like Sanjay and Anne. Why is it that some young people can use help while others seem to find it impossible? Of course, in some cases, it may be that we do not have the resources or we make mistakes, but what is disheartening is that sometimes when we believe we have come up with good solutions, they are apparently thrown back in our faces. This question brings us on to the issue of emotional development and how it affects the reaction of different individuals to the circumstances, including the traumas, of their lives.

Psychic Development and Suicide

While it is easier to see how disturbances in the environment can push young people to suicide, it is clear when we look at the differences between young people's reactions in similar circumstances that we need to understand better, their inner states that create these differences and can so complicate our attempts to reach and help them. Often these states of mind are closely linked to depression – whether or not they present as clinically depressed.

Freud compared depression or 'melancholia', with mourning (1915). He felt that both are precipitated by the experience that something has been lost. In normal mourning it is obvious what has been lost, but in melancholia the loss is often of an ambivalently loved figure which cannot be faced, and instead, the figure or object is taken in and felt as part of the self. The sufferer comes to feel as if he is the lost object, and as such, is attacked and hated, giving rise to the self-reproaches and despair of the depressive. Freud felt that instead of being able to face the separation and the inevitable guilt and anger that this provokes, the depressive 'lives forever', so to speak, with the hated object. This

69

process is rather well illustrated by a patient seen by Fancher (1972), a Canadian psychologist. A young adolescent girl's mother was murdered by a soldier with whom she had spent the night. In the ensuing inquiry it became clear that unbeknown to the family the mother was in fact a prostitute. The family then denigrated and condemned her, attempting to disown her. Her daughter refused to believe this about her mother and defended her bravely and strongly, but some two years later, she herself changed, becoming wild and very promiscuous, picking up men for one night stands. Eventually she became depressed and then took a massive overdose. Fancher's view of his patient was that rather than face a view of her mother that would have destroyed the mother in her eyes, she identified with her; she became her mother and attacked her both by the shame and disapproval she brought on herself and eventually, by enacting a complicated violence against her by trying to kill her/self. In other words, this ambivalently loved mother was taken into herself, identified with and attacked, all without any conscious knowledge on her part that this had anything to do with her mother. She felt it was herself alone. Suicide – the enactment of violence – was felt as an escape from an intolerable situation and the ultimate act of hatred against the object and the punishment for doing so at the same time. Sometimes in a tortuous personal logic, it is to save the object.

This process often has a sadistic overtone; there is gratification as well as punishment in the self-destructive activity and this sense of revenge and triumph that also accompanies much suicidal behaviour is another reason why we find it so disturbing to become involved. Anne's activities also have a ring of cruelty about them, not only against herself but also against those trying to help her, especially her beleaguered social worker who is led such a disturbing dance. 'You always come back', the social worker said, confused and depressed by Ann's actions as she returned to her office after yet another effort had failed. It is often so difficult but yet so important to try to understand what is going on, particularly as professionals, when we feel provoked like this. Anne is being cruel to her social worker and carers and yet when she does this, who is being cruel to who? Is she enacting in some deadly way her father's cruel hold over her – 'If you stand up to me, I will kill myself'. Rather than face the father's cruelty as well as the risk that he really would kill himself and so leave her with intolerable guilt, she becomes her father – identifies with him and puts her social worker, in the position of the abused child herself. In this way she also holds on to relationship with her father rather than separating from him and risking his death. This sense of terrible persecution between self and other is surprisingly also a way of never giving up a loved object. This man who abused her horribly was unfortunately the only father she had, was the person who was sometimes affectionate to her, bought her ice cream and looked after her after a fashion when she really needed him and for this reason, she can never give him up, nor can she escape her concurrent hatred of him.

Freud's view of the power of these destructive processes led him towards the view that there is a basic destructiveness within all of us which he called the death instinct, and a number of psychoanalysts, especially Melanie Klein, further developed this idea. This is the notion that the innate capacity for love is balanced by a counter-tendency towards destructiveness. Such ideas led to a development in psychoanalytic thinking away from seeing sexual desire as the main anxiety in development, to a much greater emphasis on the fear of the consequences of hatred and violence on those we love or hate. Thus a primary problem faced in development is how to manage our hatred and that of others in order to protect ourselves, and others whom we love and need.

These early experiences of very powerful emotions threaten the infant with being overwhelmed by his own violence. These feelings are dealt with by very primitive manipulations of the ego, splitting and projection, so that some equilibrium is established. A part of the self is able to remain in a loving relation to a good mother but at the price of having to ward off the knowledge that lurking in the shadows of the mind is another darker side, which is full of hatred for a mother who is also felt to be full of hatred, so that there is a recurrent threat that this other bad world can take over and shatter all peace of mind. If development goes well and the infant's own balance is more towards loving feelings and the disturbed feelings are held and calmed by a strong and loving mother, then many of these split off, violent relationship are reunited with their idealised counterpart and there is a coming together of these good and bad experiences with a resultant sense of wholeness as well as sadness and regret what Melanie Klein termed the depressive position. But when either the infant's aggression is too great, or the quality of maternal holding is inadequate or even actively hostile then these bad experiences are never reintegrated into the self and have to be dealt with in other ways. Thus where there really are bad or confused objects as in the case of Anne these may be incorporated into the personality where they constantly threaten the stability of the personality. In adolescence there is an upsurge of intense emotion and a process similar to the infantile once described above is set in motion again. Once more parents and other adults are needed to help contain

71

these feelings and when this is not possible, the underlying fault lines in the personality can give way leading to breakdowns.

Mark

A boy of 14, Mark, came to see me in an extremely disturbed state. His breakdown had begun with a row with a friend. This other boy had complained to his father and the patient feared that his friend's father would kill his own father and then frame him so that he would be held responsible, though of course he was entirely innocent. This belief gradually increased in strength and became a delusion. I thought the delusion was derived from his hostility to his father which he attempted to deal with by disowning it and locating it in the other man – the friend's father. But instead of being able to gradually face this hostility and deal with his guilt about it, he was quite unable to do so. His anxieties escalated and instead of just one danger, he started to believe he was now surrounded by hundreds of Afghan rebels who he was convinced were trying to kill him and actually were poisoning him and breaking his legs. He was very upset that 'they' were also attacking his father and mother, and in addition killing hundreds of people whom he was sure would turn up as bodies in his home. It was as though this bad father (not his, but his friend's father) had now become fragmented, disseminated into a wider and wider world so that each fragment, as it were, became another bad father – the Afghan rebels. Moreover, his perception of this badness and danger had become quite bizarre. While in the room with me, he believed that a siren, from a passing police car outside my window, was evidence that the enemy were after him. Noises in my room became evidence of listening devices. Running through all this the thought was that others were dying because the killers were unable to reach him, but his death would put an end to all this suffering even though it was undeserved. He imagined that he might have to sacrifice his own life to save the world or possibly even his parents to save them from torture.

This is an illustration of the primitive anxieties about death and destructiveness, and the primitive feelings of possessiveness, love, jealousy can, if not worked through early in life, remain dormant and when there is a later upheaval, say, precipitated by some crisis or perhaps the changes of adolescence, these primitive feelings break through and dominate the personality leading to violent upheavals which in certain people, can lead to self-directed violence. I felt there was a real risk of suicide in this boy. Of course not all failures of parental containment will lead to a psychotic breakdown as happened in Mark's case. He was clearly suffering from schizophrenia or a schizoaffective disorder which needed to be urgently treated but his symptoms still conveyed a clear meaning and the power of his impulses may well have been the precipitating cause of the breakdown even if there is a biological aspect to his vulnerability to breakdown in this way.

Conclusion

Why is it that some people can bear these surges of primitive anxiety within themselves when others seem precipitated towards impulsive action? I would like to say something about the question of communication and containment of anxiety, since this is so central in the work that we try to do with these distressed young people. Wilfred Bion was a very important Kleinian analyst and has been referred to several times in this book. He came to the view that in early life, the baby achieves a sense of psychological holding and safety by having a mother who can be in a state of openness to the baby's state of mind called reverie. The baby can, and indeed must, communicate primitive anxiety to the mother who, in a quite intuitive way, drawing on her own inner resources including her past experiences of maternal care, receives these feelings. She copes with them, is open to them, is affected by them, but is not overwhelmed by them. There may be all sorts of experiences – a primitive fear of dying, for example, of course not an adult version, something that we recognise, but something which we could only approximate to our adult language, something like a stomach-chilling fear, a sense of nothingness, a sense of disintegration, of everything being lost. Such fears are induced in the mother and felt sometimes quite acutely – 'Is my baby dead? I feel terrible', etc. If the mother can manage such fears, then she communicates this back to the baby in her own language – the tone of her voice, the manner of holding, a look in the eyes, and the baby then has an experience of relief, of someone who could manage something that he cannot. Gradually, after many experiences like this, the baby can learn to tolerate primitive states of mind. Thus containment functions as a way of detoxifying the baby's primitive experiences. When this fails either because the mother could not be sufficiently available in this way or because the baby was not able to use the mother's capacities, then instead of developing a sense of internal safety and security, the baby retains a fundamental anxiety and a tendency to react strongly when insecure; other methods are used which often lead to action. It is as though by putting these fantasies into

73

action, there is a sense of ridding the self of a dangerous world. It is better out than in, is the philosophy, and the whole intolerable situation that threatens the self is now safely outside it.

Mark, the 14-year-old boy, was probably faced with an anxiety of murderous feelings towards his father and fears of retaliation coupled with intolerable guilt. In his version, he is free of guilt, it is not he who threatens his father but another man (the friend's father). There was a sense that this process had been escalating through the preceding year and now the fear was that there were hundreds of deaths, the violent forces against him were so great that he was in a state in which it eventually seemed to break down his whole self and the experiences were no longer felt to be within his mind, but to be quite concretely going on in the external world which of course, brought him relief at a terrible price of real terror for his life. Clearly what is missing or has broken down in Mark is any sense of the possibility of containing his fears of violence. By now, there was only one communication possible really, by Mark, and that was that he needs us to know he was overwhelmed by his anxieties and that he should be in a safe place. He said many times that our outpatient clinic was not safe for him and I think he was right. The way to help him at that point was for him to get a sense of someone knowing what a state of terror he is in and that the response of moving him to a place where he felt safe would be the only way in which he could feel he was being taken seriously. What I mean is not simply to consider what is the right decision but also, how to convey to him that we have heard him and his fears and we have understood that he is overwhelmed and in need of a safe place to recover his mind.

This sense of needing someone to know about disturbed feelings is one that is commonly felt by adolescents. As I mentioned earlier it is clear from epidemiological surveys that family stresses, deprivation and parental difficulties are important factors which predispose the individual to depression and suicide. This is because adolescents especially often require the presence of adults who can be responsive and react appropriately to help them through periods when they are experiencing primitive anxieties. Adolescence is a time of enormous change. It is ushered in by far-reaching physical changes of both developing sexual maturity and rapid changes in size and shape. This leads to the need to develop a new identity, to develop new relationships, including sexual ones, to face increased potency and power, to face separation from home. All of these changes mobilise considerable anxieties especially if early development has left some primitive fears untouched or unworked through. If the anxieties are not too great and there are responsive adults available, then it is possible for many adolescents to work through these experiences which can often include feeling depressed and transiently suicidal. If their feelings become overwhelming there is a combination of their severity and the absence of containing parents, then the sense of inner containment breaks down and can result in action of some kind or another – sometimes violent behaviour, sometimes behaviour that is more depressive and self-harming. It is often at these points that professional help is mobilised. Sometimes the professional is required to supplement what has been absent in the family, thus with Sanjay, the first example, it was possible for him to draw attention to his plight and with a combination of foster care and psychotherapy he was able to settle down without recurrence of his suicidal feelings even though he is still, not surprisingly, a very troubled young man. In the case of Anne, however, something much more disturbed had developed within her so that the very process of trying to contain her, seemed to provoke in her a combination of feelings of inner claustrophobia and an outward cruelty towards anyone trying to help her, making this task enormously difficult. This essentially arising from her impossibly ambivalent feelings about a father whom she both hated and loved and who she cannot free herself from. What was very striking with Anne was the way in which she does *mobilise* other people. There was a strong sense of communication but it seemed she could only use the people who heard her to enact her unresolvable conflicts.

In some patients, the process of attacks on the self can form a closed system inside the self which in some of the most serious cases, does not lead to the communication of anxiety at all. If they do come to professionals, there is often a sense of non-communication and it requires great persistence to get them to open up and then to be able to discover the seriousness of their disturbance. These are the kinds of patients, and they are relatively rare, who constitute the greatest suicidal risk. Some never seek help but apparently suddenly, and out of nowhere, commit suicide. Piecing together the events leading up to their tragic actions does sometimes reveal signs which in retrospect should have been taken much more seriously. Sometimes families and professionals are faced with the disturbing realisation that an apparently calm person was planning an unequivocal suicidal act and not revealing it in any way. There will sadly occasionally be cases where it is not possible to prevent a suicide. Some of them become involved with suicidal fantasies in an idealised way, planning and thinking about death for long periods of time. This becomes a secret way of life and eventually, these plans are carried out. This kind of psychopathology is often, but not exclusively, found in patients suffering severe depression.

Sylvia Plath

I want to quote from two poems by Sylvia Plath, who after making several very serious suicidal attempts referred to in this first poem eventually took her own life. She was a depressive who explored this process in her poetry in a harrowing but often moving way. She had the capacity to express so eloquently what most people in this state do not and cannot communicate. The first, which captures this fascination with death, is called 'Lady Lazarus':

> I have done it again.
> One year in every ten
> I manage it –
>
> A sort of walking miracle, my skin
> Bright as a Nazi lampshade,
> My right foot
>
> A paperweight,
> My face a featureless, fine
> Jew linen.
>
> Peel off the napkin
> O my enemy.
> Do I terrify? –
>
> The nose, the eye pits, the full set of teeth?
> The sour breath
> Will vanish in a day.
>
> Soon, soon the flesh
> The grave cave ate will be
> At home on me
>
> And I a smiling woman.
> I am only thirty.
> And like the cat I have nine times to die.
>
> The second time I meant
> To last it out and not come back at all.
> I rocked shut

76

As a seashell.
They had to call and call
And pick the worms off me like sticky pearls.

Dying
Is an art, like everything else.
I do it exceptionally well.

I do it so it feels like hell.
I do it so it feels real.
I guess you could say I've a call.

She also had some insight into the origins of this state which was probably closely related to her passionately ambivalent feelings about her father who died when Sylvia Plath was only nine years old. This is from her poem 'Daddy':

If I've killed one man, I've killed two –
The vampire who said he was you
And drank my blood for a year,
Seven years, if you want to know.
Daddy, you can lie back now.
There's a stake in your fat black heart.
                                    Sylvia Plath (1962)

It's a terrible image of her relationship in her heart to this father which most people with her kind of difficulties could not describe so vividly, and yet it is not unfamiliar in those whose ties to their closest figures also consist of a cruel, unrelenting attack on each other's hearts. Only by murder could he be stilled like the ancient response to suicides, but the only way to carry this out is by killing herself, since her love for him means he must live on in her heart for ever. This is the vicious cycle of melancholia.

All those who work with severely suicidal patients are faced with a real burden. We are frightened, provoked, filled with anger and sometimes even hatred. We are made to feel responsible and guilty. There is of course no way round this often bewildering and upsetting situation, but when we can find some measure of explanation that can make sense of why some of our clients or patients behave as they do, I do think it can take some of the sting out, the pain of pointlessness, and it can of course get us to make better decisions which can sometimes be lifesaving. Small comfort, perhaps for much of the time, but then expecting too much of ourselves in such work can become a burden not only to

77

ourselves, but to our patients. Somewhere they usually know how difficult they are and simply being understood, withstood and tolerated may be a rare experience for them and if we are patient, the grip which their negative states of mind have over them can gradually lessen and they can learn to tolerate themselves better.

References

Alvarez, A. (1971) *The Savage God: A Study of Suicide*, London: Weidenfeld and Nicholson.

Brent, D.A. (1997) 'Practitioner Review: The aftercare of adolescents with deliberate self harm', *Journal of Child Psychology and Psychiatry*, 38: 277-86.

Fancher, R.E. (1973) *In Psychoanalytic Psychology: The Development of Freud's Thought*, pp. 207-10, Noton New York: London.

Freud, S. (1915) 'Mourning and Melancholia', *S.E.*, xiv.: 237-58, London: Hogarth.

Shaffer and Piancentini (1994) 'Suicide and Attempted Suicide', in Rutter, Taylor and Hersov, *Child and Adolescent Psychiatry, Modern Approaches*, Oxford: Blackwell Scientific Publications, pp. 407-24.

Plath, Sylvia (1987) 'Lady Lazarus', verses 1-7 and 13-16; and 'Daddy', verses 15 and 16, line 1, in *Collected Poems*, London: Faber and Faber, (written in 1962).

Shakespeare, W. *A Midsummer Night's Dream*, Act Three, Scene II, lines 380-7.

6

Reflections on Some Particular Dynamics of Eating Disorders

Gianna Williams

For a number of years, I have been assessing, treating or supervising a large number of patients suffering from eating disorders. I have become interested in certain features that seemed to recur in one particular subgroup of these patients, namely those who have been or, at least, have experienced themselves as recipients of parental projections.

One of the patterns I noticed repeatedly was a defensive rejection of input often not confined to food intake, but extending at times so widely that it might be referred to as a 'no entry' system of defences (Williams, 1994 and 1997). I shall clarify this point with reference to one patient in whom this pattern of defences was particularly extensive.

Sally, a severely anorexic Afro-Caribbean girl who was 17 when I first assessed her, told me that her mother had died of alcohol abuse when she was 13, and that she used to be a very frightened woman – always terrified of drowning in the bath tub – and she asked her daughter to hold her hand when she was having a bath, when Sally was still very little.

Sally was referred because of severe anorexia, but I was confronted, in her assessment, with a vast array of 'no entry' defences. Sally was maintaining her weight just above the 'severely at risk' level because she had a terror of being hospitalised and tube fed. She had been treated twice for dental abscesses, under general anaesthesia, because she would not accept to be given an injection in her mouth. She could not bear the sound of the alarm clock, nor the sound of the telephone. I felt, in my countertransference experience, that it was necessary to speak using a soft tone of voice and to use 'pastel' rather than 'primary colour' types of words.

Sally was horrified at the thought of any sexual contact, let alone penetration. She was reluctant to be touched *on* her skin during a medical examination.

When I started treatment with Sally, she conveyed the unrealistic hope (Potamianou, 1997) that I could somehow exorcise her of all her terrors. She utterly denigrated somebody she had seen previously for a brief period of psychotherapy: 'A bull in a china shop ... certainly born under the sign of Taurus'. As for me, I was idealised as someone 'certainly born under the sign of Libra'. She knew for sure that the likes of me never lose their temper and read 'The Guardian'.

We tend to understand persecutory anxiety as the consequence of a fear of retaliation from sadistically attacked objects, also as a consequence of excessive projective identification, but the extreme and pervasive dread of being invaded and intruded upon in 'no entry' type of patients like Sally may also be related to early very persecutory experiences of being at the receiving end of projections perceived as inimical. I have often noticed in my countertransference that 'no entry' patients can break and enter into me with powerful projections of an intensity that parallels their dread of being invaded. A highly concrete example of this early in Sally's treatment occurred when she demanded to know if I had a panic button near my armchair. When I asked why, she said in a menacing voice, 'What would you do if I threw acid on your face?' I felt temporarily blinded by the impact of this projection.

Later projections continued to be powerful, but gradually they acquired a more symbolic dimension. In his paper on counter-projective identification (Grinberg, 1962), Grinberg pointed out that an experience of being heavily projected into in the countertransference should alert the clinician to the possibility that the patient might himself have been at the receiving end of massive projections.

In my own experience, this seems to apply particularly to patients who have developed 'no entry' defences against being projected into rather than those who have remained 'psychically porous' and open to parental projections. I do not find that 'porous' patients project as heavily or frequently as 'no entry' patients.

In recent years, I have attempted to deepen my understanding of 'psychically porous' patients who suffer eating disorders and who tend to be more frequently bulimic than anorexic. These patients seem to bear an intriguing similarity with those described, from a different perspective, in recent child development research, as belonging to a fourth, new category of attachment, the 'disorganised, disoriented' pattern of attachment (Main and Solomon, 1986). According to Main's extensive research, children who have developed this pattern of attachment have been exposed to the experience of parents who had themselves suffered traumas in their lives and who were either frightened or frightening or both. From a psychoanalytic perspective, frightened or frightening parents are likely to project anxiety rather than contain it (Bion, 1962).[1]

When projections enter a child's psychic space, they can be experienced as very inimical *foreign bodies*. I wish to emphasise that I am not focussing, in this paper, on the predicament of patients who receive back their own projections, which is the predicament described by Bion (Bion, 1962) as 'nameless dread'.

A mother who cannot deal with her own psychic states will indeed send back the child's projections, but I wish to focus on the experience of patients whose parents need to divest themselves of *their own* anxieties, psychic pain, and ghosts (c.f. Fraiberg et al., 1975). It is a failure in the relationship between container and contained which is, in my opinion, even greater than the one described as engendering nameless dread; a failure of containment of a second kind.

I would like to reflect on this predicament by describing in some detail my work with a bulimic male patient who had remained highly porous indeed to parental projections.

Daniel

Daniel is a boy who had the experience of *literal foreign bodies seeping into his blood stream* when he was still in the womb, as he was born addicted to Valium. Daniel had not developed a system of defences of the 'no entry' type and had remained very 'porous' to projections.

He was eighteen when I started seeing him. He was, at the time, severely bulimic. I saw him initially non-intensively and, gradually increased his sessions to four per week.

Daniel told me, in his first assessment session, that he was born 10 weeks premature and that his prematurity had caused a number of malformations. For instance he had 'two large bumps on his head'. They were probably oedematous and they receded when he was still in the incubator. He also had non-patent nostrils, a frequent feature of prematurity. He referred to them by saying that he had 'no holes in his nose'. His nasal tract was operated upon many times, the last time when he was 4 years old. As he had 'no holes in his nose' he must have been fed in the incubator by a tube passing through his mouth. Mother was told by the doctors that there was no hope that he would survive and apparently gave him up for lost. She became pregnant with a 'replace-

81

ment baby' (Reid, 1992) when Daniel was still in the incubator. There were only eight months between the full term date of Daniel's birth and the birth of his brother Julian.

Daniel is an attractive boy of average size. Both Daniel, Julian and a third brother Tommy, five years younger than Daniel, spent repeated short periods of time in a children's home when Mother was admitted to hospital for psychotic breakdowns. On one occasion she was admitted after trying to set fire to the house. The family moved to London from the North of England when Daniel was twelve and his parents separated when he was thirteen. Father died recently from a drug overdose. He was a builder, often out of work because of serious problems of alcohol and drug abuse. When under the effect of alcohol and drugs, he was violent to Mother who was hospitalised several times.

Mother had also been hospitalised at the age of 15 when she became severely anorexic. She subsequently developed bulimia. Daniel too had become anorexic at the age of fifteen and subsequently bulimic. He told me that when he was anorexic he used to live on one apple and one coca cola per day. His weight had gone down to 41kg. He had been very ill, missing more than a year of schooling. He had not been hospitalised, but put on medication by his GP. 'Like his mother', he said, he had switched from starving himself to bingeing and vomiting. He told me early in treatment that he knew he was going to re-live every step of his mother's life and that she had told him so. She was sure that he was *just* like her.

Daniel was certain that, at some point in his life, he would be admitted to a mental hospital like his mother, and that he would be cleaning lavatories like her when he was 45.

When Daniel felt haunted by the ghost of, (in his words), 'falling into the groove traced by his mother', he seemed oblivious of his areas of functioning and comparative freedom, such as his academic achievements which were considerable in spite of the schooling he had missed, and his current serious eating disorder.

Describing his bulimia, Daniel conveyed a vivid perception of being full of inimical foreign bodies. When I started seeing him he was bingeing and vomiting up to 6 times a day. He was tormented by concrete bodily feelings, of being 'all dirty inside'. Blocked sinuses and nose contributed to his perception. He said he felt 'greasy', 'full of soot', 'disgusting'. Vomiting gave him very temporary relief.

He binged on anything he could find or buy with his limited pocket money allowance. He bought mostly loaves of white bread which, he said, was 'like blotting paper'. It soaked up 'all the nasties' which could

82

then be got rid of by vomiting. After being sick, he felt temporarily 'clean inside'. His mind became clear and for a few hours he could apply himself to his studies. Then 'the buzz', as he called it, would start again. When 'the buzz' started, Daniel was unable to concentrate. He would press the wrong keys on his word processor, sometimes erasing a file that he wished to put on the memory. He described 'the buzz' as 'thoughts racing through his mind at 150 miles per hour'. It became clear that they were not thoughts he could think or talk about, but something more akin to flying debris.

When Daniel searched for food to binge on, he described himself as 'running around like a headless chicken'. He put across a feeling of fragmentation and utter despair. Strikingly, he neither binged nor vomited at college or when, occasionally, if given free entrance, he went out with his friends to a disco. It only happened at home.

The First Period of Treatment

Daniel was highly receptive to his mother's projections and he perceived home as a very unsafe place. He had, nevertheless, a few good memories from his childhood in the North of England.

He recounted to me a beautiful or, rather, idealised memory. He might have been 4 or 5. It was a sunny Christmas day. The sky was blue. Mother had told him that angels come down from the sky on Christmas day and he had visualised the white angels against the blue sky. He could still see the picture in front of his eyes. 'At that time' he told me 'I felt that my mother was an angel'.

I said that he now often spoke about his mother as if she were a witch and that he seemed to perceive me as some sort of an angel who had come down from the sky to rescue him. I tried to put across with the tone of my voice that I felt somewhat uncomfortable about my angelic status. I attempted to share with Daniel this fairy tale picture. Witches and fairy godmothers, witches and angels: they belong together. Daniel said on one occasion, with a laugh, that there was a sentence about angels in a song he liked very much. He told me some of the verses:

> You are just like an angel ...
> I wish I was special
> You are so very special,
> but I am a weirdo
> I am a creep.

Daniel was not only idealising me during this initial period of treatment, but he was also, to some extent, making a bid for *mutual* idealisation.

Sadly, his mother had told him on a number of occasions that when he was born he was the 'ugliest thing on earth'. He was *so* deformed that she felt unable to look at him, especially after his brother Julian was born: a normal baby.

Daniel needed to feel that I did not perceive him as a 'weirdo or a creep'. I experienced in the countertransference that Daniel had the notion of an object that could accept him and perhaps even like him. At other times I felt a strong request for fusion and denial of any boundaries.

Daniel said that when he lived in the North of England, he would go for long walks by the coast every day. He knew the time of the tides and would sit in a cave at low tide, staring at the sea. This description evoked a chilling feeling in me as I felt that Daniel might have wished to be swept away by the sea. The wish to merge with the sea also brought to my mind his having been evicted prematurely from the maternal womb.

The theme of the sea and of a wish to merge with it continued when Daniel started talking in some of his sessions about his fascination with Melville's Moby Dick, a text he was reading for his exams. It is interesting that Daniel never spoke about Captain Ahab or the whale, despite their central role in the novel. Instead he only spoke about Ishmael and his irresistible attraction for the sea.

Daniel needed to impress me for a long time with literary quotations. He told me that his academic achievements were the only thing his mother was proud of. When in primary school, he was so good at maths and spelling that the teacher would stand him on a table and get him to answer questions about multiplication and the spelling of difficult words. I repeatedly interpreted, with a query in my voice, the conviction conveyed by Daniel that he would matter little to me if he were not so good in his studies.

Once he told me that he *knew* he was not very interesting or enigmatic, just a 'textbook case'. So he felt he 'needed to buy my interest'. In the same session he quoted from a novel by D.H. Lawrence. He told me of a woman who idealises a man and the man is frightened that she might someday 'see the darkness through the petals'. No darkness was allowed to cast its shadow over our relationship. At the beginning of treatment Daniel was only able to locate the darkness, not even shaded by petals, in his relationship with Mother.

His bid for mutual idealisation, which I repeatedly, gently, but steadily, tried to interpret, needed to be accompanied by interpretation of persecutory anxieties which could only be firmly anchored to the transference when the first Christmas holiday approached.

Before I describe the difficult time prior to the first Christmas break, I would like to give a glimpse of Daniel's description of his room in Mother's flat. I think this might help in understanding some aspects of Daniel's reaction to what he perceived as my abandonment.

Daniel described his room at home, which he shared with his youngest brother Tommy, as a hopeless bomb site. He described it as if he wished me to make a home visit and help him to concretely sort out the mess.

Only the little table where he did his homework was kept tidy. The table faced a window. When Daniel was studying, he could forget about the debris behind him. One important aspect of the debris was a pile of clothes. Mother washed and dried Daniel's and Tommy's clothes in the washing machine, but she put them on the floor of the room, in a pile, expecting the boys to sort them out. Jeans, socks, jumpers, underwear were described like a sandhill out of which Daniel and Tommy would extract some items, but neither of them could be bothered to put some order into the pile. Daniel told me about this unsorted pile of clothing, for the first time, in a session when he had arrived to the Clinic wearing odd socks.

I think it is important not to overlook a contributing factor in the mess, namely the resentment that Daniel experienced as he expected that Mother should have sorted out the clothes for him, just as he made me feel, in the countertransference, that I should have concretely gone to his home and helped him to tidy up. He seemed to be asking me explicitly to perform this function at a more mental level when he wrote to me, on a Thursday, a letter which I would receive prior to his Monday session. It said:

I have only seen you today and I am already here writing. I am sure that you are sick of me. I have read almost every minute since our meeting. I have started reading Plato for my essay, then I remembered that I had not finished the Joyce book I was reading, so I left Plato and I started reading Joyce. It is now 11 at night. I have read a little bit of Plato, a little bit of Joyce, I have almost finished Wilde's amazing *Portrait of Dorian Gray* but I can't remember very much about it. Then I started reading Plato again, but I can't stay with anything. If I could come to a session tomorrow, you could help me to find some rhyme or reason in what is happening.

Such sorting out or filing was crucial to Daniel to provide some rhyme or reason in his mental and emotional life. I was aware of what an important part of my job description this was.

Returning now to the 'room/bomb site', Daniel had told me that the 'worst thing was the door'. It was always ajar as the handle was broken. 'A missile', he said 'could always come through the door'. I asked Daniel, if he could give me an example of a missile coming through the door. He said it could be 'Mother barging into the room and telling him that she was going to kill herself because she had found out that he had been bingeing again' and that she knew 'he was never going to change'.

By now, Daniel's eating disorder had slightly improved. He was now able to go two or even three days without bingeing and vomiting. It returned with a vengeance after I gave him the dates of my Christmas break: a real missile through the door.

The First Long Break

I told Daniel about the dates of my holiday many weeks prior to our last session, so that we would have plenty of time to work through his reaction.

His bulimic symptoms returned in full force and suicidal ideation was present in his material. For instance he made a reference to his mother having attempted suicide a number of times; once it happened at Christmas. I told him explicitly what I felt he was conveying to me.

Daniel spoke about the effect that he seemed to have at home, on his mother and his brothers: 'I am getting them all down, their moods depend on how I feel in the morning'.

On a day when he felt very desperate, his mother had given him a poem that she had copied from a book. He told me the poem made him feel 'really like quitting'. He wanted me to keep the poem, so I would understand what he was talking about. I will quote the poem as I think it contains a number of significant 'foreign bodies'. At this point it was a clear transference communication about my being, for Daniel, an object unable to tolerate projections and returning them as missiles:

> I will succeed. I simply cannot fail.
> The only obstacle is doubt
> There's not a hill I cannot scale
> Once fear is put to rout
> Don't think defeat
> Don't talk defeat
> The word will rob you of your strength
> 'I will succeed'. This phase repeat

> Throughout the journey's length
> The moment that 'I can't' is said
> You slam a door right in your face
> Why not exclaim 'I will' instead
> Half won then is the race
> You close the door to your success
> By entertaining one small fear
> Think happiness talk happiness
> Watch joy then coming near.

The message was clear. I was going on holiday because, like Mother, I could not tolerate Daniel's gloom and depression and bulimia. He felt he was too much for his family, too much for me and, I think, as a consequence, too much for himself. He was unusually cynical in his rage about my abandonment. 'If I killed myself', he said, 'it would give a kick start to my family'. This did not feel like an empty threat. He certainly meant to give a kick start to my holiday break.

A history of suicidal thoughts emerged during this time. Thoughts which I had seen adumbrated in the phantasy of being swept away by the sea, when he was a child. Daniel repeatedly expressed his vote of no confidence in me. He arrived for a session after a weekend, looking like a neglected stray. He had a heavy cold and the skin above his upper lip was red and chaffed. He said that I could not understand how he had been feeling and how he felt. 'The weekend had been hell, bingeing and vomiting all the time.' If I had not been in hell myself, I could not possibly understand.

I interpreted during the weeks prior to the break that Daniel felt I could not possibly take a break and leave him, if I *really* understood how he felt, if I knew how often he 'felt like quitting'. Maybe I did understand, but I could not take it. I was going away because he was too much for me.

My countertransference at this time was not only bearing the impact of a threat that 18-year-old Daniel may die. I was being required to experience the anxiety that Bion considers most central in the containment of an infant: 'The fear that the baby may die' (Bion, 1962). As you may remember, Daniel had been given up for lost at birth. At that time the anxiety that he may die was bypassed by a certainty that he would die. I took Daniel's suicidal threats seriously and arranged for emergency cover which fortunately was not needed.

Something on the side of life was mobilised in Daniel during the work preceding the holiday. He decided to spend the duration of my Christmas break at the house of his friend, Nigel, whose parents were going away for a 'holiday in the sun'. Daniel told me that however miserable he was going to be at Nigel's place it was going to be better than spending Christmas at home. Mother was, at this time, very depressed and was saying that Daniel was getting her down with his bingeing and vomiting. Father, Daniel told me, was likely to turn up just to scrounge a Christmas dinner. Father, he said, was *so* greedy.

By staying at Nigel's house, Daniel was running away from his suicidal mother and greedy father, perceiving them as intolerable and inimical foreign bodies. Yet it was striking how identified he was with these intolerable objects, before the holiday break, in his own suicidal ideation and bulimic pattern.

I wish to emphasise at this point that the intolerable quality of the natural parents was not only due to their projecting into Daniel. As internal objects, they were overwhelmingly persecutory as they were passionately hated by Daniel. He perceived them as incapable of performing a parental function. At this particular time – Christmas – they were carrying a great deal of the rage and hatred evoked in Daniel by my abandonment of him.

During the break, Daniel did not binge or vomit at Nigel's house. He only did so when he went, on three occasions, to his mother's flat to collect some books, tapes or clothes from the heap on the floor.

Daniel was sorry for Nigel who had been left alone with his older brother at Christmas while the parents were having their 'holiday in the sun'. It was clear, on my return, that I had been equated with this abandoning, unconcerned sexual couple who knew of better ways to spend the festive season than listening to the moaning of a child.

The 'Nigel's parents' type of couple was provocative, but certainly an improvement on the suicidal mother and addicted father. I find Henri Rey's (1994) suggestion that patients bring their objects to analysis for them to be repaired very apposite to what was happening at this stage in Daniel's treatment.

The Missile in the Transference

The separation and feelings of abandonment had been a painful, not a shattering experience for Daniel, but I was not easily forgiven for my holiday. Not long after I returned, he had a dream which conveyed poignantly his feelings of exclusion and of curiosity:

He was sitting on the top deck of a bus. He was somewhere in North London, possibly Hampstead. He was looking into houses. It was probably evening because the lights were on. He saw people sitting round the table, parents, children, families.

Daniel was sure that I lived somewhere near the Clinic in a very middle-class area. The subject of middle-class and middle-class children became an arena for the venting of resentment and bitterness. On one occasion, talking about a rich middle-class boy at school who affected a cockney accent, he said: 'I really pity the middle classes, they have to try so hard not to be hated!'

He told me about an essay he had written. In the essay, Daniel spoke about a West Indian boy, Winston, who suffered from sickle cell anaemia, an illness not found in the genes of white people. Winston resented the health, the privileges, the easy life and the flaunting of John, a boy who lived in a five storey house. (The Clinic where I work has 5 floors.) Winston had cast a spell on John who had contracted sickle cell anaemia. In the essay, Daniel had described John's mother's distress about her son contracting such a severe illness. I felt it was amazingly transparent, but it came as a total surprise to Daniel that it might have something to do with my 'middle-class children'.

It is interesting that this disturbing essay was based on a phantasy of introducing, by magic, sickle shaped cells, indeed 'foreign bodies', into the bloodstream of my envied privileged child.

The theme of sibling rivalry has been central in my work with Daniel. Not surprisingly, given that his brother Julian (a middle child) was conceived when he was still in the incubator.

I would like to quote briefly some material from a session not far from a holiday break which gives an opportunity to observe, within the transference, Daniel's ease in perceiving himself as a receptacle of projections.

Daniel had become increasingly interested in modern art. He often binged on visits to galleries, now that his actual bingeing and vomiting had reduced. He told me about a painting he had seen at the Tate Gallery called 'The Dancers'. On the left side there are couples cheerfully dancing. This aspect was described by Daniel in detail. On the right side of the painting there is a precipice. This was said almost in passing, as if I should not notice it. When I remarked on this and made a reference to the precipice, Daniel reacted angrily, saying, 'I don't need you to talk about the precipice. I think about the precipice all the time. You don't need to remind me'. Daniel obviously felt as if I was projecting 'doom and gloom' into him, a depressed mother reminding him that 'happiness never lasts'. I interpreted this perception: Daniel was thoughtful. After a pause, I wondered whether there might not be a different way to think about the painting, in the context of our forthcoming break. The precipice that he wished me to ignore might have something to do with the feeling of being dropped that he generally has when there is a break, when I, like the dancing couples, waltz away from him and he thinks that I forget him.

This particular interpretation seemed to greatly lessen Daniel's feelings of persecution. It is a characteristic of the transference, when working with patients who have experienced themselves as receptacles of projections, that the initial reaction to some interpretations, cautious as they might have been, is akin to the perception of a 'missile coming through the door'.

I think that it is only by working through this experience again and again in the transference relationship and helping the patient to modify his perception, that a change in the internal object can gradually take place and a process of detoxification of foreign bodies can be set in motion.

Wish to Possess and Control Foreignness

During the spring term, Daniel tried to find out the origin of my first name. He had seen this written in full on the letter offering him his first appointment and had been told by a friend of his who had been to Mallorca that I was probably Spanish. He was sure I was going to spend my Easter break in Spain.

Shortly before I left for my holiday, Daniel met a foreign girl, Maria, with whom he fell in love, almost at first sight. By the time I came back from my holiday Daniel and Maria had become 'inseparable'. This was not solely a piece of holiday acting out: the relationship has lasted and it is still going strong.

Daniel felt passionately attracted by Maria's foreign accent, by her foreign mind and her foreign 'unbelievable ways' of being at home with her feelings, so different from anyone he had ever met before. 'It humbles me', he told me, 'the way she can show her love for me'. Daniel was full of admiration and a certain amount of envy and jealousy for Maria's mastery of foreign languages. She was fluent in English, Spanish and Danish.

Daniel became involved in learning Danish. He gave me an example of what he could manage to say in Danish in the early days, to show me how far he had moved. He could say 'simple things', like: 'I am sad' 'Why are you sad?' 'Because no one takes any notice of me'.

Daniel was able with much effort to let Maria catch a glimpse of 'the darkness through the petals', and to tell her about his eating disorder. This occurred once it was, by the summer of the first year of treatment, 'a thing of the past'. Maria was at first shocked, but this new perspective also helped her to understand why Daniel had still to go and see 'that precious woman at the Clinic'. Maria was at first jealous of Daniel's relationship with me. She was often used by Daniel as the spokeswoman of all his doubts and mixed feelings about therapy.

Daniel's mother, in turn, did not take kindly to his moving out of the flat to go and live with Maria a few months after he had met her. I interpreted Daniel's communication that all these women were fighting over him with their inordinate possessiveness. He certainly no longer felt that he was 'the ugliest thing on earth'.

Some 'missiles through the door' continued to materialise in Daniel's life. As the network of his relationships became wider, it was, at times, difficult to draw material into the transference. I shall give an example.

After he had moved out of his mother's flat, she kept ringing him, often leaving messages with Maria if Daniel was out at college. One day Mother insisted she needed to talk with him urgently. Apparently she needed to tell him that he had been seen in the street by two people she knew and trusted, who said that he looked as if he were on drugs because he walked about 'like a zombie', with his mouth open.

Daniel was indignant about this accusation of addiction. He said Mother was mixing him up with his father. He had plenty of troubles, but alcohol and drugs had never been one of them. If there was one person in the world who should know why he was walking about with his mouth open, that should be his mother. The reason for keeping his mouth open was the only partly successful operation on his nasal tract. There was something objectively provocative in mother's accusation, and I had no reason to doubt Daniel's truthfulness. I think it would have also been provocative to disregard Daniel's feelings about the reality of his physical difficulties and to only make a beeline for transference interpretations.

Slowly Daniel and I began to think together about the sensitive area that had been touched upon in him by this event: namely his own anxiety regarding addiction. Something that had come to him as the unbearable projection of a foreign body could perhaps be given some meaning through thought.

Daniel was aware that the pattern of bingeing on food had been replaced by compulsive reading. He would go from one book to another, keeping three or four books going at the same time. There was a difference from the bingeing and vomiting pattern in that something

91

of what he read did stay in his mind and got into his bloodstream. This was to be witnessed by his exam results which were excellent.

Daniel would probably have been hurt by Mother's phone call in any case, but he was hurt in particular because he *did* feel anxious about his tendency to develop addictive patterns – notwithstanding the less harmful one concerning literature. A dream helped us to explore his fear of addiction in the transference, at a time when I started talking about the possibility of a third session.

> Daniel was in the waiting room at the Clinic. There he met a boy, a friend of Nigel, who is actually also attending the Clinic. The boy, Sean, asked Daniel whether he had ever tried Guinness. Daniel answered with vehemence that he didn't want to try anything alcoholic. Sean had insisted that he should really try Guinness. Daniel had been persuaded and he had tasted it. It was *so* delicious, he said, that you could not describe it. He felt in the dream that he could have easily become addicted to it and want to have it *all the time.*

When he woke up he didn't know, for a while, whether this had actually happened or whether it was a dream, just as in the past he had at times dreamt of bingeing and had woken up unsure as to whether it was a dream or reality.

Daniel had some associations to the delicious taste of Guinness. He said it was not at all like the taste of beer which he disliked. It was creamy, a little like Horlicks (a sweet bedtime drink). This is an interesting association for a child who had never been breast fed, even worse, who had been fed for the first weeks of his life with a tube passing through his mouth and going directly into his stomach. A preconception about the heavenly quality of mother's milk, creamy and delicious like Horlicks, seemed to have remained alive in his mind.

The theme of how addictive a taste of a good thing could be for him, recurred in the period when I was able to increase the number of his sessions.

I was again encouraged by Daniel to see Mother as responsible for all evils. He told me she had phoned him and said that she wished to buy shoes for him and Maria. He had not been able to resist, although he didn't want to accept the offer. Mother had 'spent a fortune' on expensive shoes. Daniel resented the fact that his greed was fanned by this type of experience. Mother knew this and always knew how to make him feel greedier, while he was trying to control his greed.

The metaphor offered by Mother's 'unwanted generosity' was fairly transparent in terms of my offer of an extra session. It was not difficult, in this case, to work on the issue of an object projecting and evoking feelings of greed with apparently generous gifts. Daniel's greedy wish for 'more Guinness' (which is as near as you can get to my first name), wanting, in his dream, to 'have it all the time' first became clear after I increased the sessions.

His reaction to a gap in the middle of the week, when I didn't see him on Wednesday, was marked. He felt that gap in the week to be the 'worst hole', worse than the one at the weekend which he said he had got used to. On a Wednesday, he got himself locked out of his flat. He had left his keys at home and Maria, who had the other set of keys, was not going to be back till late. He wandered through the streets of London, stopping in a cafe to read a book for a while before wandering again. While walking in a lonely street he had found himself crying. There was a mixture of sadness and resentment when he told me about this 'horrible Wednesday'.

His perception of wanting more and of missing his sessions shifted, later, to a characteristic pattern *in the Thursday session*, the last one of his week. During one of them, Daniel put across a tremendous feeling of urgency and I reflected on the fact that he was interrupting me all the time, as I was trying to talk with him. I wondered whether this had anything to do with it being a Thursday. He interrupted me again: 'Oh yes, Thursday, I know I grab more on a Thursday. I feel I've got to get it all in 50 minutes because it's the last session of the week and I know I will not get it all in a session and I always feel that whatever you say is not *the answer* and then I feel: "So what do I do now, what do I do now?".' In the same session he said that he felt 'wide open, anything could get into him'. It was evident that he perceived the experience of separation as a projection of pain into him – a transference equivalent to 'the missile through the door'.

I had opened Daniel to more pain with each offer of an extra session. Daniel somehow felt he had to protect himself from this experience. He had never worn a watch since I had known him, but Maria had given him a watch with an alarm as a present on his birthday. On one occasion, I heard a little bleep a few minutes before the end of a Thursday session. Daniel said it was 'because sometimes I tell him that it is *nearly* time to go, but sometimes I don't'. The bleep from Daniel's watch was a little disrupting in the session, but I did not experience it as an 'attack on linking' (Bion, 1959), as it conveyed a message loaded with emotional meaning.

I would like to conclude the clinical part of this paper with a brief reflection on different types of countertransference experiences in work with patients prone to attacks on linking mainly driven by envy, and with those predominantly struggling, like Daniel, with the disruptive effects of experiencing themselves as receptacles of projections.

We are all familiar with the painful and, at times, provocative countertransference experience evoked by patients who are devoted to disrupting our thinking in a session. Attacks on linking are a popular defence against the psychic pain of knowing 'where it hurts and why it hurts'. A patient I wrote about many years ago (Henry, 1974) who has been equalled by few in his capacity to undermine my capacity to think in a session, could not tolerate, for a time, my beginning a sentence with the words: 'I think ...' He sometimes covered my voice saying 'You think, you think, you are a brain box' disrupting my thinking before he knew about my thoughts.

My work with Daniel has not been totally immune from attacks on linking, but they have been a comparatively rare occurrence, in spite of his difficulty in differentiating my putting him in touch with *his own* psychic pain from my injecting a 'foreign body' into him. I have been confronted and I am confronted, most of the time in my work with him, with a countertransference experience that is very different from the one I have with patients who are very devoted to attacks on linking.

I have not forgotten Daniel's essay on sickle cell anaemia, but I do not think that he is a predominantly envious patient. I have often perceived in him a feeling of relief and of sincere curiosity about his mental life, when something I said made emotional sense to him, when it lessened his confusion or detoxified a disturbing 'buzz'. You may remember that, when he described his room in Mother's flat as a bomb-site, I felt that he was asking me almost concretely to make a home visit and provide some order.

This appeal seemed to be very similar to the one in the letter cited earlier where he said: '... if I could come to a session tomorrow you could help me to find some rhyme or reason'. Daniel described himself also as persecuted by 'thoughts flying through his mind at 150 miles per hour' (not really thoughts, but debris). He needed me to help him to give a name and to put some order into his states of mind.

I am reminded of a beautiful metaphor used by Esther Bick in the supervision of a psychotic girl I treated intensively well over twenty years ago: 'Your attention to everything she does and everything she says acts like a magnet that draws together the fragments of her personality. Have you ever seen a magnet drawing together iron filings? That is what a mother's attention also does for a baby'. Esther Bick always spoke about babies whatever the age of the patient. If I reverse

Esther Bick's metaphor, I could say that Daniel was asking to be rescued from the experience of being at the mercy of a 'wind scattering iron filings'.

At this point I would like to refer to Bion's (1962) description of the vital developmental function of an object that is capable of receiving the projections of feeling and discomforts a child cannot himself give a name to or think about. The containing object receives the projections and attempts (sometimes successfully) to give them a name, modify them and make them thinkable. This Bion referred to as Alpha function or Reverie, and it can only be performed if the containing object bears the emotional impact of projections and makes 'emotional sense' of them. When referring to the predicament of a child whose projections are not accepted, Bion says that such a child, exposed to the experience of an impervious or impermeable object, receives back his unprocessed projections in the shape of 'nameless dread'.

The case I have described was one of a patient who was used, almost always unconsciously, by one or both his parents as a *receptacle* of their projection, *their* own unmetabolised feelings or 'ghosts' (Fraiberg, 1975).

I have been asking myself whether it would be useful to attempt to formulate a hypothesis about the function performed by an internalised projecting object. Bion says that the introjection of a parent capable of containment or performing Alpha function helps a child to internalise a function that links and organises thoughts and feelings, and makes order in his internal world. Could one say that the introjection of a parent overflowing with projections has an obverse function, namely a disorganising impact, in the internal world? (Cf. Main and Solomon, 1986).

When a patient introjects a projecting object, it might be useful and justifiable to formulate the hypothesis that this projecting object also performs a function. A function which is the obverse of Alpha function, not in the realm of the negative grid but at the opposite end of the alphabet. Namely, a possible 'Omega function'.

Daniel's experience of thoughts flying in his mind at 150 mph could be seen as due to the presence in his internal world of this disorganising, disrupting function. It seems appropriate to use the term 'function' in this context because I do not think that the meaning of this word should be confined to the positive. There is no doubt, for instance, that terrorism performs a function, albeit a disruptive one.

I have been drawn to attempt to formulate a hypothesis about the particular interference with thinking in patients who have been recep-

95

tacles of projections because the countertransference they evoke, as I said earlier, is markedly different from the countertransference evoked by patients who are intent on attacks on linking.

The message one receives in the countertransference when working with 'porous' patients like Daniel is: 'Please help me to tidy up. Please help me to differentiate foreign bodies from what is nourishing and to internalise a filing system, an organising function of my own'.

I would like to conclude by saying that the internal landscape of a child may show craters where the foreign bodies have landed, but around these craters there may be a desolate volcanic terrain or a devastated bomb site, or there might be at times, as in my patient Daniel, soil that has been able to nourish growth, in spite of craters. There might be some live and enlivening internal objects that inhabit the internal landscape and mitigate the inimical nature of the foreign bodies.

Notes

1. In my work, I rely extensively on Bion's concepts of 'container' and 'contained'. However, when dealing with patients who have been at the receiving end of projections, I have found it better to use the terms 'receptacle' and 'foreign body', as there is no actual container and, therefore, nothing is contained.

References

Bion, W.R. (1959) 'Attacks on linking', *International Journal of Psycho-Analysis*, 40: 308-15.

———— (1962) *Learning from Experience*, London: Heinemann.

Breuer, J. and Freud, S. (1895) *Studies on Hysteria*, S.E.2, London: Hogarth Press.

Fraiberg, S., et al. (1975) 'Ghosts in the nursery: a psychoanalytic approach to the problems of impaired infant-mother relationships', *Journal of the American Academy of Psychiatry*. 14: 387-421.

Grinberg, L. (1962) On a specific type of countertransference due to the patient's projective identification. *International Journal of Psycho-Analysis*. 43: 436-440.

Henry [Williams] G. (1974) 'Doubly deprived', *Journal of Child Psychotherapy*. 3(4): 15-28.

Main, M. and Solomon, J. (1986) 'Discovery of a new, insecure-disorganised/disoriented attachment pattern', in *Affective Development in Infancy*, (eds) M Yogman and T.B. Brazelton, Norwood, NJ.: Ablex Press, pp. 95-124.

Potamianou, A. (1997) *Hope: A Shield in the Economy of Borderline States*, London: Routledge.

Reid, M. (1992) 'Joshua – Life after death. The replacement child', *Journal of Child Psychotherapy*, 18(2): 109-38.

Rey, H. (1994) 'That which patients bring to analysis', in *Universals of Psychoanalysis in the Treatment of Psychotic and Borderline Patients*, ed. Jean Magagna. London: Free Association Books, pp. 229-249.

Rosenfeld, H. (1987) *Impasse and Interpretation*, London: Routledge.

Williams, G. (1994) 'La sindrome "Vietato L'accesso" (The "no-entry" syndrome)', in Quagliata, E. ed. *Un buon incontro* (A good encounter). La valutazione secondo il modello Tavistock. (Tavistock Model Evaluation). Roma: Casa Editrice Astrolabio, pp. 140-53.

——— (1997) 'The "No Entry" System of Defences: Reflections on theAssessment of Adolescents Suffering from Eating Disorders', in *Internal Landscapes and Foreign Bodies: Eating Disorders and Other Pathologies*, London: Duckworth, pp. 115-22.

The Fear of Becoming a Man

A Study of Two Adolescents

Hélène Dubinsky

Introduction

The sense of self develops through emotional experiences which begin in early childhood. At the start of adolescence, the young person is confronted with major demands which will test out his or her sense of self. Adolescence itself is a time of growth and of turmoil, confusions and great vulnerability. In order to continue developing their identity, adolescents need to separate from their families. They usually seek reassurance and assert their emerging identity through belonging to a peer group.

Physical and sexual maturation may offer a promise of taking one's place in a new generation of grown-ups, which will be 'better than the parents'. This exacerbated wish to be better than the parents rekindles the infantile (Oedipal) competitiveness with both the parents and siblings. Feelings now so powerfully re-evoked in adolescence may be for example 'I want to be stronger and more powerful than my father', or 'I want to be more attractive than my mother and be a better mother than her' or 'I want to be the favourite child'. Entering the grown-up world confronts the adolescent with a profound sense of inadequacy as growing up requires actual achievement, such as passing exams, establishing sexual and emotional relationships, becoming able to take responsibilities for oneself and those that one loves, often in the context of unbearably intense feelings. Understandably, adolescents often feel unequal to the task. States of mind in young people often oscillate between helplessness and inadequacy, (feelings which are inevitably increased by the rivalry with their parents and siblings) and feelings of omnipotence (which gives them an exaggerated sense of their abilities).

This chapter is intended to give a more inside view of the way we

99

think about and speak to our young patients. It reflects the intensity of the work with those who are experiencing a temporary but acute sense of 'a world gone mad'. This kind of upheaval is not unusual in adolescence. It can be deeply disturbing and lead to a state of temporary mental breakdown. Nevertheless experienced professionals can be of great value to help young people to think about the strange and irrational world they find themselves in when bodily changes coincide with a series of profound emotional shifts.

In this chapter I have looked at the psychotherapy of two adolescents, who I have called Julian and Thomas. For them the struggle to become 'men' seemed an impossible and frightening task. Through detailed accounts of a session with each of them I hope to illustrate some of their deepest anxieties about growing up, and being able to emulate their father and their siblings. Both Julian and Thomas had felt they needed to divest themselves of a competent and masculine part of their personality in order to jettison some of their aggressiveness which was felt to be too destructive towards themselves and those around them. They withdrew into their own shell and were trapped for some time in a regressed childlike state. One could say they both seemed to have withdrawn for a period of time into a state of temporary madness.

Before starting treatment Thomas suffered from panic attacks and was unable to leave his house for several months. As for Julian, he had stopped attending college and for two years his obsessional fears forced him to live as a recluse. Although both were in a desperate situation and stuck at home, there were important differences between these two adolescents.

Thomas despised men and he felt 'cursed' by his masculinity. This left him incapable of any achievement and he saw himself as totally inadequate. He feared he would end up as a tramp. At the same time he had a deep longing to be loved and understood. These longings became confused with his overwhelming desire for a total fusion with a girlfriend.

Julian's level of disturbance was more severe. While Thomas was suspicious of all men, Julian's suspicions had a more delusional quality. He believed that there was a particular boy walking the streets, waiting to beat him up, humiliate him and deny him his right to be a man. All his emotional energy was consumed with this excruciatingly painful obsessional thought. As a consequence his emotional life and interests were narrowly restricted.

100

7. *The Fear of Becoming a Man*

Julian

Julian was 19 when he started once a week therapy with me after referring himself because of his history of school phobia and breakdown in his college attendance. With great difficulty he tried to recount some details about his past. He told me that he had had a happy childhood and that his parents are nice people with whom he gets on well. His sister was three years younger and was successful in her studies. It emerged that when he was younger he had suffered from obsessional anxieties because he had to wear glasses. He had done well at school but eventually his sister overtook him academically. He then began to have difficulties in going to school and for a while he stopped attending. He did manage to go to college when he was sixteen, made some friends, and he felt he was 'free at last', as he put it. Then the 'incident' occurred when a boy from another school attacked him in front of the college, knocked him down and punched him. Julian let himself be beaten up without fighting back and to his added shame it was witnessed by a crowd of other boys at the same college.

Soon afterwards Julian abandoned college and his studies. He stayed home for several years out of fear that he would again meet this boy somewhere and be beaten up if he went out. He was possessed with this thought at every hour of the day and he held onto to it with an almost delusional intensity. Eventually, a few months after starting therapy, he was able to return to his education and he restarted college.

During the first months of his therapy Julian was tense all the time, often looking sullen and distrustful. He would say little, then in short explosive outbursts say something like 'there is nothing to say, "he" is always there.' It was impossible for him to 'open up', or to drop his guard in case the boy would attack him. Julian felt threatened when I tried to understand the meaning of his obsession as if I was trying to make him give in to it. It took almost a year of therapy before Julian could begin to talk more freely, to smile at times, or even feel he could trust me more. However, he had managed to venture to college and was able to take his exams even though he only revised for them in the last few days. One of the exam questions was on a topic that he had prepared for and he was tremendously pleased; he felt he had been lucky at last.

I will now give a detailed account of a psychotherapy session at this time.

Julian began the session by saying it had been an awful week and said he had only managed to do some work at the beginning of the week and no more. With a knowing look he added that it didn't help that his sister was going to university. I acknowledged that it was painful for him to see his sister being successful, leaving him feeling jealous. He agreed but reminded himself that he had been 'lucky' in passing one of his exams, a feeling that for once fate had privileged him. However, he was angry, his therapy was only 'once a week and this was just not good enough'. The waiting between sessions seemed so long and made him feel small, helpless and angry. When I commented on how much he hated these feelings, he smiled and began to talk about a football game that he was hoping to go to. He had desperately wanted England to win four years ago but they lost and it had been a terrible disappointment which had greatly affected him. Now, in a similar situation, he didn't feel he would be so obsessed as he had once been. I could talk to him about his growing awareness that the struggle to do well was happening here in his therapy and also in his college work, where he was more willing to take a risk in studying even if he didn't always get the results he wanted. Julian added that four years before he was just going along with school, now he was taking it more seriously. Nevertheless, he said: 'It's alright here but when you step outside there is a chance of meeting him (the boy)'. I commented that we both knew the incident had taken place, but that this boy was also still in Julian's mind, sneering at him and in particular, at the part of him that felt small and helpless. Julian's reply was bitter: 'it hit me as I was becoming an adult, he was there around the corner'. His comment conveyed how strongly he felt someone had stopped him from becoming a young man on his way to achieving his potential; instead it had turned into an obsession. Julian argued: 'if I get rid of it, if I send it way (referring to his obsession with the boy) then I am not me anymore. I wish I was free but I'm not. It happened.' I tried to show Julian that he had created a prison inside himself where he was trapped and at the mercy of somebody who robbed him of his strength. To be free would mean he was able to work, to make new friends, and to get on with his life. Julian responded to my comments: 'I can never have a whole picture of myself because he is there. I wish he was dead and he wouldn't be in the picture. I could do without the fear.' He continued, 'the picture is a fantasy, there isn't a perfect picture, is there? I have to acknowledge that it did happen, don't I?'. Julian listened carefully when I pointed out that the whole picture included not only a small, frightened, helpless child and a boy who triumphs over him but also a part of Julian that could be strong, be thoughtful and who could struggle and fight back. Once the incident happened, he had lost touch with that part of himself.

Julian then brought up a conversation he had with a Muslim boy at school who had tried to convince Julian that the Koran is the truth, and he concluded that these people are dogmatic. Here I tried to show him how he was dogmatic when he gave in to the belief that the boy who beat him up had ruined his life. Julian said in a reference to Salman Rushdie that God 'wouldn't sanction the killing of a man, would he?'. I talked

102

about the fundamentalist aspect of him that felt he, Julian, was 'a sinner, was bad and a failure', and how these feelings made Julian feel doomed and an outcast. Julian agreed, saying: 'I am doomed, I wish I had something I believed in, but I don't'. I suggested that he did wish he could believe in the therapy as a relationship where one is not passing judgement, or being dogmatic, but where thinking could take place and where the needy and frightened child could be accepted.

Julian said 'if there is a God he would want you to do the best for yourself and others'. I commented on his longing for a paternal figure who was just, understanding and who didn't turn people into outcasts. I talked also about his wish to do his best now, and Julian agreed but said 'I'm afraid to be myself in case he comes up and slaps me. I don't want to try and fail and fall.' His fear of taking the risk of becoming involved in our therapeutic work was apparent because he was frightened to fail, to be slapped down or to be abandoned. Julian went on to tell me that things had been much easier when he was a child, everything was black and white and he had felt safe: he said that he was scared and asked how could he know if the good, strong part of him could stand up to the boy? He went back to the incident, remembering that there was a crowd of boys around them and that they were all on the boy's side. 'You can die in a fight', Julian said, 'I was so shocked and my image was destroyed completely.' I commented how, then and now, it was difficult for Julian to remind himself that there was a side of him that did have the capacity to stand up for himself. It was time for the session to end and he left with a rare smile.

After this session Julian stopped talking about the other boy and in the following weeks he became more aware of how worried he was about studying because of his fear that he would fail and not get the results he felt he deserved. He also talked about his great fear of examinations, and he began to express some interest in girls. Terror was beginning to make room for less paralysing anxieties and more ordinary preoccupations.

Comments

Julian's father was in fact a rather successful man, and I think Julian felt a tremendous feeling of rivalry towards him, which in his somewhat fragile family he had been terrified of expressing. His own struggles and his capable sister stirred up murderous feelings in himself which he could not bear. The 'other boy' who so blighted his life not only served to represent his father, whom he felt defeated by, and also a disarmed part of himself which was so destructive. It was also a realisation of Julian's wish to give up on his own development so that his constant obsessive preoccupation became a substitute for really facing up to his difficulties. I often felt his obsession had quite a secondary gratification for him, since it so defeated his parents and of course my own wish to help him. Through this process he both weakened his personality by divesting himself of his power while increasing his helplessness – which in turn made his persecutors more powerful. As he began to perceive his need to see a whole picture of himself, Julian is more able see how crucial it was for him to bring together these aspects of himself – a bullying part, a capable and strong masculine part and a helpless childlike part – in order for his emotional development to resume.

Thomas

Thomas was 17 when he was referred to the clinic for severe panic attacks which had stopped him from going to school. He had become practically house-bound following his first panic attack a year earlier. This first attack occurred after he had been looking at photos of his deceased grandmother when she was young. Several panic attacks followed a few months later after taking large quantities of soft drugs with his group of friends. By the time he came to the clinic, he felt his whole world had fallen apart, he was depressed, scared all of the time and he could see little point in life.

Thomas was keen to accept my offer of individual psychotherapy. I saw him for four years, twice a week during the first year and then once weekly for the remaining three. When I first met him, I was shocked by his physical appearance. He was extremely thin, his face was a sickly grey and his very long uncombed hair hung down to the middle of his back. Although it was a cold day he wore a skimpy jacket, and there were huge holes in his trousers. He looked like a tramp and produced a deep impression of physical and emotional misery. He seemed to be in a state of complete disintegration. He cried during most of the assessment sessions, telling me how he could not cope, and how everything felt too much. He just wanted to lie down and sleep. At the end of each of these meetings he begged me not to throw him out.

Gradually, as Thomas recounted his childhood, the events which he felt had precipitated his breakdown emerged. His childhood with his mother, father and sister who is five years younger than him, had been very happy. He described feeling close to his divorced grandmother whom he had 'idolised'. As a child he felt: 'the whole world revolved around me. My mother and my grandmother were part of me and I looked up to my father. He was strong, always right, he was the leader'.

Then when he was about ten years old, his father left the family for another woman. A few months later his much loved grandmother suddenly died leaving Thomas haunted for years by the image of her body in the coffin.

Death, ugliness and a tremendous sense of unfairness and loss seemed to have suddenly invaded Thomas' world, and he felt everything worthwhile had collapsed. It was as if he had lost 'his backbone' when his father left, and he said: 'When my parents divorced and I was alone with my mother I felt I had to grow but I didn't really grow, just inwards, like ingrown toenails'. Referring to the loss of his grandmother Thomas said: 'my childhood ended when she died and the whole of me died'. He described how his mother became out of touch with and persecuted by her children's needs. Although he managed to maintain contact with his father it was a further blow for him when, shortly after his parents' separation, his father lost his job and remained unemployed. Communication between father and son became difficult and Thomas stopped admiring his father. He would often say that at the age of ten or eleven he was suddenly required to grow up. Meanwhile his mother had re-married and Thomas felt unmitigated hatred for his step-father. He also talked about his hatred of his grandfather whom he described as an uneducated, angry and argumentative person.

For a long time Thomas used his therapy to pour out his depression, his mal de vivre and his complaints about a whole range of ailments which included dizziness, sore eyes, exhaustion, and an imaginary brain tumour. In this way he seemed to want to fill me with those same feelings. He was lost, drifting aimlessly, depressed and close to falling apart, but there was also a self-indulgent and omnipotent side to him in which his blaming and raging about all the 'shit in the world' had a triumphant and gratifying quality. Thomas' moods constantly oscillated between manic elation and depression. I also noted that while he was often self-destructive in his therapy he could also be sensitive and personable. At times he showed his appreciation that all these feelings had a place here and that we could begin to think about them together. For a while Thomas seemed to live between his bed and the therapy room, but he gradually returned to school for a few hours a week and he was able to do an A level in Art, while still complaining bitterly of feeling ill all the time.

Besides a deeply ingrained conviction that he was too ill and too fragile to cope with life, Thomas also had a deep hatred and contempt for men which he often expressed in a categorical refusal to be a man. For example, he would say about his step-father, 'my mother sees him as charming, I see some beast. I feel sheer revulsion for him. He is diabolical, a creep, he is wrong, he is evil, he might poison us all'. And about men: 'I don't feel like a man. Men are macho; men are powerful and strong, but in fact they are stupid. The world is run by men. They become hardened when on their own. The only way for men is to be loved by a woman, it's all they have got. Women are the real power and wisdom.' Moreover Thomas did not feel at home in his own male body: 'my body is not my own, perhaps it is my father's or somebody else's'.

After some time Thomas resumed his nightlife, which included going to clubs with his friends and drinking, although he now stayed off drugs, aware of the danger for him. He talked about feeling part of the crowd and at the same time a complete outsider, pretending to be a 'bloke' but feeling old, ugly and inadequate. He desperately wanted a girlfriend but thought it was too late. He was frightened he would 'jump in' and that 'it would become an obsession', recalling a previous attempt at a relationship where he had so idealised the girl that he felt his own personality had been quite lost. He was so identified with women that he felt his feminine attributes were what would attract girls to him. 'Everybody's after my hair', he would tell me, 'I want to cut it but I may lose my appeal'.

Following a Christmas holiday, Thomas described a party where he met Kate, who became his first girlfriend: 'I was talking to this girl. We talked and talked in a corner and she told me that I was really nice and asked if she could be my girlfriend. I said no but I really wanted to tell her that I would love her forever. She asked me to kiss her and I said no and when she asked me why I told her, because I had to make it clear, "I am not a man". She was nice though and said she hoped that I would get over whatever it is that I am going through'. Thomas was terrified of being disappointed. He said: 'if I kiss someone, I don't know what will happen. I should stop myself, I should save myself from something dangerous like disillusion'.

Thomas was longing to immerse himself inside the safety and comfort of the mother of his childhood, represented now by Kate. His fear of 'something dangerous like disillusion' is in reference to a terror of suddenly being turned away from something like a sanctuary. This referred to the loss of his secure family before his father left and his grandmother died. Behind it lay earlier experiences of being close to his mother as a baby when he had felt that he had sole possession of her with no father to think about. Claustrophobic anxieties are often related to very early infantile fears of being trapped inside the mother (Klein, 1946; Meltzer, 1992). All young children are fascinated by the

106

inside of mother which is felt to contain the source of goodness and safety. At times young children really believe at some level of their mind that they can go back inside their mother in order to gain safety and comfort. It can also be a way of avoiding the painful experience of being a person separate from mother. For some children and adolescents, this defence can turn into a way of life. But because the child or adolescent is then exposed to the fear of being trapped inside, the refuge turns into a bad place. There is furthermore a fear of the revenge from all the rivals (siblings and father) who are felt to be with mother all the time.

In the case of Thomas, the desire to live in phantasy inside his mother seemed to proceed from the experience of a mother who was affectionate but not really available emotionally. This phantasy was meant to allow him to lose himself in a fusion with mother. In reality it exposed him to the claustrophobic anxiety that led him to the panic attacks.

In his view, men were always cruel bullies. This was why he preferred to see himself as a child or a girl with long hair and these thoughts led to his telling Kate that he was not a man. Despite intense self-doubt and extensive ruminations, Thomas did fall in love with Kate and they had a tender relationship, but when she wanted to make love he was petrified. During a session which I will now describe in detail, Thomas experienced intense claustrophobic anxieties. This allowed us to explore the meaning of the panic attacks and the fear of having a close sexual relationship.

Thomas started by saying, 'Kate and I have not had sex yet. Whatever I plan doesn't happen. Things happen to me, I'm not in control.' I talked about a side of Thomas that felt having sex meant taking the place of his father and of other rivals, and that this was frightening. He replied that he didn't 'want to procreate at all. One should not enlarge the human race'. I suggested this idea made him feel worried and guilty. Thomas said, 'It doesn't feel right to talk about it any more, it's wrong, wrong', and he became increasingly agitated, adding: 'I feel I shouldn't be here. It happens to me all the time. I feel OK then suddenly I have the shock of realising that things are not what I thought. It's like having a panic attack. You suddenly snap out of what you are doing and you think about things'. This, I pointed out, is what seemed to have happened here just now, and he agreed, adding: 'Yes. Listening to what you are saying, not feeling right about being here'. I went further and suggested that he had this feeling not only with Kate, but here as well when he felt close to me, in this room when we talked together about these intimate matters. He might then feel he had taken over the father's place with me. Thomas agreed: 'yes, being here. I was just coping with things, not questioning things and then suddenly something just snaps.' I said that one moment it was comfortable to be with me, that he felt like a child close to his mother. But then he suddenly feels frightened and guilty as he fears that in his competitiveness he has got rid of all his rivals here.

We could then think together about how Thomas felt like an intruder both here with me and with Kate. Thomas said: 'when I am happy I want to be a father. When I'm sad, I feel like I don't deserve to be here, that my being born is like I am an impostor.' I talked about his guilt about being born, since he thought that this meant others being wiped out. I suggested that he felt worried and guilty that he felt he took possession of the mother, or me here, and this left no room for the father, or for other siblings, the other 'babies'. With bitterness, Thomas agreed, saying: 'Yes, I'm depriving them – I know what competition is – I'm OK, stuff them, fuck off, I can get all the milk'. He added: 'you have to look after yourself, because my mum is just a kid. Kill or be killed, this is how people live'. Thomas was showing me, how in his mind, he either kills the father and the other 'babies' or he is their passive victim and he is killed. Therefore, one has to be tough because there aren't any real parents around.

Thomas' response was to identify with the victim and he said: 'that's what I can't get over. I can't ignore everybody's suffering. I should be doing something, I should be Jesus – he died for everyone. He wasn't the son of God, he was an anguished man. He saw all the shit. I feel the same way'. Here we could see the omnipotent side of Thomas, in that he had to rescue all the victims in the world to make up for the fact that he could not believe in the idea of his mother's (or my) capacity to care for him and give him the protection he needed. This lack of trust was particularly marked as we were approaching the summer break.

Talking about having sex with his girlfriend made him, in an almost delusional way, feel as if he had succeeded in getting inside the mother, a thought which on its own could induce a panic attack in Thomas. Sitting in the therapy room and being emotionally close to me made this experience of intrusion feel concrete. His feeling that he 'shouldn't be here' was an indication of his fear of the strangeness of the experience and of his guilt over his ability to take over the place of the father and of other siblings, (real or imaginary) for that special place inside mother/me. His aggressiveness, needed to overcome his rivals, has to be quickly projected somewhere else; in this instance, into what for Thomas is his mental image of a bad father. This leaves Thomas back on the same side as the victim. Finally in a manic and grandiose manner he sees himself as a Christ-like figure left to repair the damage caused by a sadistic father and rival siblings.

Thomas' urge to intrude and seek refuge in phantasy by being over close to a mother appeared to proceed from a lack of trust in good parents. This lack reflected his experiences in earlier life when his father left home, his grandmother died suddenly, his mother became emotionally unavailable for him, and his new step-father was felt to be cold and unsupportive. The longing for a 'lost paradise' was further fostered by his belief that as a child before his father left, his 'mother and grandmother had been part of him'. His early enmeshment with mother and grandmother is reflected in the way he seemed to lose himself in the first girl he was attracted to, and in the way he longed to feel safe, like a bird in a nest. Moreover, such a non-differentiated early relationship had left him especially fragile in the face of the task of becoming a separate individual.

Thomas' view of the world, of men, and of life in general was highly influenced by his experience of himself as a frightened interloper who longed to creep back into a haven from which he felt excluded. During this period of his therapy Thomas was spending most of his time lying in bed or going to clubs, feeling ashamed and under a constant threat, rather like a Kafka character.

Then Thomas had a dream that the Moon was going to crash into the Earth, which a scientist told him would destroy the Earth. From our thinking about this dream it seemed very much to capture his fear that intercourse with his girlfriend would allow a primitive terror to be realised. The terror was not only of the danger of fusion with his mother but also of an end to his lifelong repudiation of the idea that his father's intercourse with his mother, which threatened him with such a feeling of danger. Perhaps the collision of these two entities separated since the origin of the Solar System also represented Thomas' fear that actually to make love with his girlfriend he would have to face that maleness was really and unequivocally part of him. He feared that this new identity, now including his father, would be fatal to him (see Introduction, p.3).

A few weeks later Thomas and his girlfriend made love. Their relationship seemed to be very tender but also over-dependent and anxious. Thomas had been overwhelmed by the intensity of his feeling and his fear that he would fall into a state of fusion with his girlfriend. Behind his fear was indeed the anxiety of a primitive re-awakening of infantile passions with which he was still very much involved since they had never been properly integrated with his external life. After the holidays he said: 'one side of me is euphoric, happy, the other side is despairing, crushed and everything is falling apart. When I'm in one state of mind I can't remember the other. Sometimes' he said, 'I think I'm schizophrenic.'

The threat of another breakdown became very near to being realised.

Thomas was accepted at an art school which he hated. The work was too much, and he felt he could not cope. He thought the male teacher criticised him, and he took it badly, saying they were all pigs. At home he was getting more angry with his mother and her partner, even threatening to kill the step-father. He dropped out of art school in a state of rage and collapse, and soon afterwards he came to his session in a disintegrated state reminiscent of the beginning of the therapy. He said that he was having a breakdown, that he could not cope and that he didn't want to go on trying. Instead he wanted to go to a mental hospital. He cried and complained that he couldn't manage to sleep any more; he was scared and depressed. 'I have a hollow core...I'm completely screwed up. I forgot that I even love Kate.' Thomas was aware that he was in danger of losing all his good feelings, and for several weeks he needed me to hold on to his hope for the future and some belief that he did after all have the strength to overcome this crisis.

By the end of the second year of the therapy, he applied to a prestigious art school, this time for a foundation course, and was accepted. A few weeks later he decided not to take up the offer because he realised he did not want to be an artist. He felt that he had never developed, or learned much and had instead wasted his education. He wanted to go back to school and start again, this time to get a real education. 'Perhaps', he said, 'I will have pleasure in learning'. He enrolled in a college to do three 'A' levels. At the beginning he had great difficulty. He wasn't used to concentrating or making an effort. People around him were younger than him, but he was able to settle down. He appreciated his teachers help and support.

Another crisis came when his relationship with Kate broke down just before she was about to go to university. Although she had found someone else the actual difficulty seemed to be more to do with having to face the pain of separating and the break-up revived all of Thomas' rage, despair and bitterness. He did not collapse this time and they were able eventually to remain friends. Thomas worked hard for his exams and took a summer job which required hard physical work. By the end of the summer he was able to leave London and begin his university career.

There were external factors which helped Thomas to develop and grow. Eventually his mother and step-father did separate and she found a new partner. Thomas was fond of this new man in his mother's life, who didn't actually live with her. His perception of his grandfather changed and he was able to talk with affection about his old fashioned common sense. They now did gardening together. The degree Thomas had chosen to do combined essential aspects of his mother's and grandfather's professions. By the time Thomas started college, he had cut his hair to shoulder length and was wearing it neatly in a ponytail. Just before stopping the therapy he went further and had it cut shorter. By then he looked like a young man, but his face still betrayed a great sensitivity, bordering on fragility. He expressed great anxieties about stopping the therapy and how he would cope on his own, but there was also a sense of excitement and adventure.

In one of his last sessions, Thomas was looking forward to starting his summer job, and he talked about his form tutor who had helped him to get the job. He felt that his teachers had been very helpful and that they were really 'nice men'. In his enthusiasm he added that coming here 'was the biggest help'. He felt that this was the right time to cut his hair and said ' I used to feel that my hair was me'.

The restoration of a good image of the father was central to the establishment of Thomas' sexual identity. This image had collapsed when his father had left home and lost his job, but it seems likely that it had always been very fragile. In his adolescence Thomas had identi-fied with a pathetic and fragile male figure. He projected his rage and violence into bad, 'macho' men. Until he was able to integrate his feelings enough, his refusal to identify with men pushed him towards effeminacy, to his view that he was not really a man. This left him only able to identify with girls and women whom he idealised. Accepting that men, like his male teachers and his mother's partner could be helpful, that firm limits were necessary, further enabled Thomas to internalise a paternal function. He was also able to recognise how the more frightening and predatory aspects of maleness in himself were an essential part of his growing up.

Conclusion

The two young men considered in this paper had not been able to meet the demands of adolescence and make the transition to adulthood. Both faced obstacles in the path of developing into young men capable of achievement. Thomas' difficulties lay in his inability to assert his sexual identity and to establish a sexual relationship. Julian had been incapaci-tated by his obsessional thoughts about encountering the boy who had beaten him up in the past. For Thomas, men were brutes or ineffectual failures while sense and sensibility lay in the domain of girls and women. His personality was further weakened by his conflict between his rage at his incomplete state and his terror at re-integration. Julian was at the mercy of omnipotent but ineffectual parents capable of exposing him to frightening persecutors. The evolution of these patients therapy has shown that in order to resume their development as young men they needed to re-integrate parts of their personality which they had divested themselves of and they needed to develop a capacity to contain their own destructiveness, which, for them, could only take place in the safer setting of psychotherapy.

Thomas' experience also demonstrated how greater integration led to the possibility of internalising better male figures and of identifying with them. For both adolescents, the firm boundaries set up in the therapy played an important role and helped the transference to develop in relation to a parental couple. The therapy offered Thomas and Julian, who were both terrified of different aspects of themselves, the possibility to address those experiences which they had been unable to contain. Because of Thomas' desire to merge intrusively with his mother, he had been left unable to internalise a thinking containing object which could help him to cope with his parents' separation and with the death of his grandmother. Julian's early obsessionality suggests that even as a child he had not been able to contain his aggressive feelings, and it appeared that his parents could not help him when he became dominated by his terror of the 'other boy'. Thinking containment, as Bion's work has demonstrated, is a necessary precondition for the establishment of greater integration of the personality and the internalisation of good figures upon which emotional development relies.

References

Bion, W.R. (1962) *Learning from Experience*, London: Heinemann; repr. London: Karnac Books, (1984).

Klein, M. (1946) 'Notes on some schizoid mechanisms', in *Envy and Gratitude*, London: Hogarth Press, (1957).

——— (1957) *Envy and Gratitude*, London: Hogarth Press.

Meltzer, D. (1992) *The Claustrum, An Investigation of Claustrophobic Phenomena*, Clunie Press.

8

'Is Anyone There?'

The Work of the Young People's Counselling Service

Elizabeth Oliver-Bellasis

The Young People's Counselling Service was set up in 1961. It was a voluntary counselling agency available to any young person without the usual formal referral procedure. At the time it was unique in both its nature and its emphasis on informality. Once open the service grew fast and six years later it had outgrown its voluntary status, the importance of its work was recognised and in 1967 it was invited to join the Tavistock Clinic and become part of the National Health Service. The YPCS of today is positioned on the boundary of the Adolescent Department. It offers a separate, confidential and limited service of up to four meetings and provides an opportunity for young people between the ages of 16 to 30 who have an emotional or personal problem they would like to discuss. This age range extends over the adolescent process that is, from middle adolescence when the 16 year old is beginning to recognise and take responsibility for difficulties within him/herself to the 30 year old who will have made some choices about where he/she is in relation to the adult world. The founder's philosophy remains; that of ease of access, confidentiality, informality and for there to *be someone there* – a professional, to be available to think with a young person in difficulty. It can be the closest they will ever get to formal treatment.

Young people are asked to refer themselves and they ring to make an appointment. Although we try to see them within two weeks the wait can be longer. There is a counselling service secretary who explains the service, asks for the minimum of details and arranges the appointments. She does not go out of her way to collect information but has developed skills in screening out clients for whom other alternative services are more appropriate.

Problems can range from those of ordinary life during the transition from adolescence to adulthood to those of severe disturbance. Difficulties may relate to separation or loss, frequently there is unresolved mourning, perhaps a parental death in childhood or an abortion. Often clients come at an anniversary time. Sometimes there are other trauma such as abuse or sexual abuse. It is often the first time that this has been talked about. Sometimes there is a crisis in the present, the death of a parent or close relative, or making a life decision about pregnancy or abortion. Sometimes there are learning difficulties, such as not being able to concentrate, exam panic, career choice or a failure to make transitions. These include leaving home, the transition from education to working life, from school to further education, from O to A levels. There are also the problems in relationships with parents, family, peers, the opposite sex, sexual anxieties, eating problems, body image and of course, problems with authority. Occasionally we see clients who are feeling suicidal or who are in need of psychiatric help. Here we take action to ensure their safety. Then there are those who set out to prove they cannot be helped.

The service offers an informal, growth orientated model of work which encourages the young person in an exploration of 'where they are now' and is designed to encourage self discovery rather than dependency. The limited contract with its clearly defined beginning and end gives some protection from being overwhelmed. The work provides an opportunity for emotional difficulties to be taken seriously: it helps clients look at what is happening in their life, and ask themselves questions which can lead to identifying their strengths and understanding some of the more difficult areas.

Adolescence is essentially a time of transition when the young person is on the move, physically, socially and psychically. It is a time of high anxiety, of instability, where feelings leap into action and identity is in a state of flux. Who am I? Where did I come from? Where am I going? There is no balance – rather a sea-saw of emotions and a rapid shifting of positions slipping backwards into infancy and being overwhelmed by dependency; and in the next instant, propelled into the adult world, feeling competent and knowing everything having overtaken the parents who are viewed with contempt.

I think of the YPCS as offering a temporary halt on this journey, a place for that experience, an opportunity for a 'story from the past' to emerge as it is given time and room with a thoughtful and attentive

114

listener. The counsellor's task is to remain open to the impact of the communication no matter how overwhelming and strange it may be, and be aware of the underlying anxiety. At the same time the counsellor needs to retain a consultative role in order to make an alliance with the 'self observing part' of the young person that is able to think about him/herself and his/her relationship with others. This provides an opportunity for change. It is challenging work for the counsellor in which I draw on my training in observation. It is work which would be overwhelming if I did not use my countertransference feelings to inform me of where the anxiety is, so that, once located and named, it becomes available for thought.

In brief work it is particularly important to go at the client's pace and be alert to the feelings below the surface even if they need to remain there. Countertransference feelings can be very uncomfortable as the counsellor uses her own experience as a traveller to recognise the signposts which may well include disturbing and hence mislaid memories. Trying to look at discomfort in oneself, to work out what is you and what is the client is the essence of the work.

There is a particular group of young people who have not only embarked on the journey we call the adolescent process which bridges the child and adult worlds but they and/or their families have made another journey, a geographic one, often halfway across the world. This journey has meant leaving the home base, extended family and country of origin to live and work here. Here cultural issues reflect and highlight the adolescent process itself as these young people are faced with a double task, that of bridging the two worlds in adolescence and the cultural history of two different countries. Imran, Sharon, Tariq and Maria are four such young people.

Imran

A young person's route to the service is often complicated. Some, like Imran feel sent, pressured by parents, teachers and other professionals in whom the anxiety and concern is located. Imran, a well-built 17 year old, arrived with an ultimatum from school. His head of year had said 'a few counselling sessions or you're out'. He wanted to go to university but had failed his mock A levels. He had come 'touched' by the head of year's concern but 'indifferent to counselling'. In his first mock exam he had been doing well when suddenly, half way through, he panicked, found he could not think, could not stand it and had left. He had arrived late for the second exam without the necessary texts and almost

115

immediately left. His problems were presented in educational terms and I was to understand that he was lazy and did not work. I was invited to view him as stupid. He told me that he had managed to get by up to now, but that 'A' levels had found him out.

Imran, the fourth child in a family of six, was born in this country and brought up on a council estate where there were a number of other Pakistani families. He conveyed a feeling of warmth and belonging both within the family and their immediate community. When he was 8 the family moved to their own house in a more affluent, middle-class, predominantly white area with better schooling. At first he had been intensely isolated and lonely – an outsider to the white world of privilege but one which he saw held all that he wanted. 'I learnt to speak properly, I got in and wanted more.' From this position of 'being in' he looked back and down on his family of origin, despising it, hating their deprivation and poverty and denigrating his parents' sacrifices. This way of getting in to 'the good world' and out of 'the bad world' meant overturning parental values and the abandonment of his family.

When Imran was 12 his parents returned to Pakistan for a holiday suggesting that he came with them so that he could learn something of his roots. Once there, they wanted him to stay 'I felt crazy'. The family returned, but difficulties with him and his adolescent sister escalated until finally, a year later, his mother and two younger siblings returned to Pakistan where they remained. This was a real loss in his life. Suddenly there were raw feelings in the room, as overcome with tears and with pain he talked of his guilt and the trouble he had caused his parents. Although Imran had not seen them for three years he stead-fastly refused to talk to his mother on the phone but remained in the room to torture himself by eavesdropping on his father's side of the conversation. Similarly, when studying, he could not concentrate, but would find himself not only missing his brother and sister, but feeding himself with their absence by playing sad music and fostering miserable-ness.

Imran said he was a good actor who could play any number of parts and that he got by cobbling things together. This meant that people did not know that he had got into a different world and that he did not belong. I felt that I was invited to be witness to his drama but only as an audience – we were to remain on opposite sides of the curtain. I asked whether it would only be the actor who came to counselling and whether we would ever be able to address the fundamental questions of who and where is he and where does he belong? I am told that he had an English first name on his birth certificate but, when he was 13 he changed this to Imran. My next intervention, though clumsy, was an attempt to reach real feeling but was dismissed as useless jargon. When I commented on this he panicked immediately, saying that his mind was blank, he had no memory of what happened and that he felt stupid. He went on to talk about his siblings, in particular his oldest brother now successfully through university and business school, and of his two younger siblings and his mother, driven to and left in exile in Pakistan – very polarised positions.

Imran's dilemma was stark. He was homesick but stuck. He could not leave this country unless he had A levels to hold in his hand as a passport ensuring his safe return. However this passport was unobtainable until he had begun an internal journey taking a step towards integration to re-find his roots where he feared he would find a mother who would overwhelm and possess him. In Imran's world there was no picture of a mother who could think about her son, who might both welcome him for whom he is, as he is, and allow him to leave her to be himself. Was it possible to bridge the two cultures and maintain links with both and could anyone be that generous to wish it for him? When I said this to him he was silent for a while and very thoughtful.

Imran did not return. He came to two of a possible four meetings, unable to complete just as he had been unable to finish his exams. I think that he could come to YPCS as long as I was ineffectual so that he could remain 'indifferent to counselling' but he could not forgive me for being effectual and providing food for thought. At the point at which he experienced me as genuinely reaching out he was furious; this was his real response to a real person. Imran dealt with his anger by cutting off and choosing instead his actor's world and chameleon existence. It left me worried and concerned about a young man who uses his mind to keep things separate so that the two worlds of his childhood and after he was nine, of mother and father, of counsellor and client, cannot meet which leaves Imran a refugee with no real sense of belonging.

Sharon

The next client, a young woman of 22, had given an English pseudonym, Sharon Jones, to the counselling service secretary. Sharon had come to the service with extremely difficult, painful experiences. These had proved so intolerable that she had dealt with them inside herself by forgetting and pushing them away and by so doing had lost a sense of herself and felt empty.

In the waiting room I was surprised to be greeted by a slight, slender, dark skinned, attractive young woman quite unlike the person I had expected. She sat on the edge of the couch throughout the first meeting beginning immediately by announcing that she had lost her feelings and wanted them back. She spoke clearly, her words in their sharp edginess conveying both a challenge and demand. As I looked at her leaning forward I had the sudden incongruous thought of a little terrier who could grip and hold on tight. It was difficult to see where this impression came from and I was shocked that I had experienced it like this. This opening was a challenge to me to look inside myself, to be curious and question my attitudes and beliefs and where I came from in the hope that I would know myself sufficiently well to be able to sort out what was mine and what, if anything, might be a communication from Sharon which evoked that picture. I was made aware that here was a young person preoccupied with her own identity who might well wish to have a fight with me over issues relating to her identity and mine. As the work evolved over the four meetings this initial startling and uncomfortable impression of who and what are you and where do you belong proved central to this young woman.

Sharon explained that in her early teens she had had a secret relationship with a boy who lived in the same neighbourhood. She had felt deeply about him but their relationship had not been sexual. Indeed, she had not even noticed what he looked like and it was only when her friends had begun to talk about him and comment on his fair hair and good looks that she had begun to think 'if he is good looking he can't have a relationship with me, I'm not good enough, I'm ugly. So I set about to do things to make myself unattractive and difficult and then we split up'.

Sharon then told me that soon afterwards this young man had become engaged to a girl who was so beautiful she could be a model. She herself had felt empty as if she had nothing inside. She had cried for months but no one had noticed her unhappiness. Apparently the boy and his family had moved out of the area but recently Sharon had seen him in the street and her feelings had flooded back, only to go again. It was after this that she had rung an all night helpline and been given the telephone number of the YPCS.

In this first meeting Sharon's painful, angry story, full of grievance, tumbled out of her as if she was trying to pack everything in and occupy all of my attention. My comments went unnoticed or were summarily dismissed making me feel that I had trespassed into forbidden territory where secrets were shut away and securely locked inside her. Just before we stopped I asked her name. She said it very quickly but it did not

118

sound like the name she had given to the secretary. She asked mine and pronounced it correctly when she repeated it. As she left she turned at the door saying 'I expect you'll forget me when you go home'.

I found myself spontaneously replying that I would not forget. Indeed I did not. I had felt myself to be in the presence of a disaster, of a world that had shattered but had been reassembled in an attempt to gain control. Her words 'I am ugly' were at its centre, providing an identity which was perversely to be valued as a defence against catastrophe and loss. My first impression of her world was of a barren and sterile one where there was no sense of life, love, warmth or the holding of real people, only the bleakness of an unresponsive world that did not see or hear. She was convinced that no-one wanted her and I too was to know what it felt like to be an outsider. I was uncertain whether she could use help.

Sharon's story gradually emerged in the following meetings. She arrived early for the second meeting carrying a large holdall. She said that usually when she met someone she gave a brief description of herself and then stopped. Coming to counselling had been different as she had found herself talking which 'was more real'. She went on to describe her visit to a club with a friend from college. When she arrived she had found the club to be full of 'blacks' and had been convinced that she was unwelcome. She continued by saying that, if she had thought, she would have been prepared for racism. A young man there had asked her out but she was sure this was only because his girlfriend came from the same culture as hers and he wanted to put her 'in that box'. She said with vehemence 'I don't want it, nothing of it, shoes, clothes, I don't want it. I know what I don't want, I'm very clear about that but I don't know what I want. I don't want to be like my mother who's at home all day like a housewife'. I thought this was her way of telling me about her experience of coming to the counselling service. I said she was making it very clear to me that she did not want to be fitted into my white box: perhaps when she had come here last time this building had looked unfriendly and boxlike. Then she had found herself in this boxlike room with a white middle-class woman with a plumy voice fulfilling all her expectations. After a pause Sharon said that she had not thought about being boxed here but she had been scared.

This acknowledgement of her feelings freed Sharon to begin to look at what had happened when she was 16. Very thoughtfully she said 'It was because everything was so painful and I didn't want it, I can remember telling myself not to think'. She went on 'I can remember saying to myself "don't think about him" and I didn't, but I dreamt. I

119

can feel in my dreams, I don't remember them but I do know what feelings are'. There followed a long, vivid description of how she had tried to talk at the time but that friends, parents, everyone, had turned away. She had been desperate and had had suicidal feelings. She told me she had kept going by taking her GCSE exams and promising herself that if she got through everything would be all right. She had passed over half but she spoke as if she had failed them all. I said how difficult it was if you split up with someone and were angry with them. You needed them to be there to let them know how angry you were. Sharon said her boyfriend's parents were racist because they kept referring to her as 'Pakki'. I pointed out that she had not told me her country of origin. She smiled saying that her parents were Indian and had come to this country from East Africa as students soon after they married in order to gain further qualifications. They were very hardworking and placed a high value on educational achievement.

Sharon started the third meeting with an announcement. She was going to break up with the young man because he was not interested in her as a person but only in a family and children. She seemed terrified of being trapped in other people's expectations and to have no picture in her mind of another person able to see her, listen, take her in and think about her inside story. I said this to her adding that she had little belief that I would recognise her and just how desperate, lost and alone she felt. I returned to my confusion about her name as it did not fit with her description of her family. She grinned slowly as if caught out but did not tell me. Instead she talked about confidentiality and the importance of no-one knowing that she had come here.

I ask her what it was like when she was little. In a matter of fact way she told me that she and her brother, a year younger, were born here, but that soon after her parents had found themselves in financial difficulty. With nowhere suitable to live, the children had been taken back to live with her grandparents, in her words, 'to live with complete strangers'. It was only two years later when she was four and a half that the family had been reunited. Although from the very beginning I had been wondering whether there had been a disruption in very early childhood which might account for the overwhelming sense of disaster, her emptiness, her secretiveness and the degree to which nothing fitted, I was profoundly shocked. I talked about the two-year-old Sharon who had felt dumped, cut off, betrayed and abandoned by her parents. This two year old had had no way of understanding what had happened and why she was in this strange place where she looked the same as everyone else but where everthing was different. At the end of this meeting I remind her that we have another and I agree with her about looking for ongoing help.

The fourth meeting was unusually difficult highlighting the problem I had had throughout to find a position where I could both acknowledge the abandoned child and at the same time locate a more adult Sharon who, in this meeting, could say goodbye and think about linking up with an agency nearer home. Sharon began it by saying that she had been thinking about last time when she had heard me suggest that the loss of her boyfriend might have reminded her of being left as a child. She spoke poignantly of a four year old who remembered her father coming to fetch them home but when he had gone out to visit friends she had screamed and demanded to follow. 'Perhaps I thought he wouldn't come back again.' 'I remember thinking what's wrong with me, what have I done.' She went on to wonder whether this was like feeling ugly with her boyfriend. Looking at me sadly she said she knew that four meetings was not enough, that she might understand but what could she do about it. She went on very quietly 'sometimes I do feel like that inside and it feels pretty desolate'. What about further help?

Sharon is one of those young people who not only do not give their address but give the service no way of getting in touch with them. In our last meeting Sharon told me the borough in which she lived and I undertook to look for a counselling service in that area. When she telephoned a few days later the counselling service secretary gave her the name, address and phone number of an agency.

Unlike Imran, Sharon was anything but indifferent to counselling. She had come disguised as if to protect herself from the catastrophe that had already happened and as a refugee from her feelings. Her way of being with me evoked a strong challenge and enlisted my wish to help. She knew what it was to have something good inside her to grip and hold on to and she was fighting to get it back.

My story about Sharon is that of a baby who could not understand, the baby who had been close to her mother but that weaning and the arrival of her brother, followed so soon by an abrupt separation from her parents had been too much. In her words 'I do think one of them should have stayed behind'. She was searching for understanding but intensely fearful that something potentially helpful would go drastically wrong.

Tariq

Tariq was 26, and at war with the world, with all in authority, with family, with parents, and above all with himself. He had come to this country on an omnipotent quest with parental blessing but had been unable to relinquish this and accept the reality of his situation. This mode of travelling arrested his development and he existed suspended between two continents with no internal parental figures available to recognise his plight. His initial phone call with the secretary had left her muddled, worried and somehow feeling that she should be able to sort out exactly what he wanted. My impression was of a sad, utterly dejected young man whose submissive manner and apologetic presence conveyed that the only way to exist was by agreement and conformity. He presented me with a list of his failures and lack of achievement stating that he had no skills and had never completed anything he started. He hotly denied being angry but went on to talk about his educational experience, one of constantly being told that he did not make the grade and moving on to find another college. There was a list of short lived attempts to get help. He made me feel hopeless and I commented that although he had come I thought he was convinced that here too was useless and that he would only return if I could provide some magic and put his world to rights. He looked ruefully at me; and I then suggested that we could think together about how he found himself in this position.

Tariq had come on his own to this country to go to university. The family home is in Bangladesh; the family are Muslim, religious but not as he put it, super religious. He was the second youngest of a family of five, in which his sister, 10 years older, had taken a lot of day-to-day responsibility for him. His mother was often ill, his father distant. Quiet and a loner in school, he seemed to have survived by slavishly emulating the good student but being constantly assailed by panic and terror that he wouldn't be able to do the work. 'Had I heard of freak out?' In adolescence he had rebelled, telling me he just did not care. To his surprise he found he worked better and had done well in his exams. In the face of stiff competition, he had won a place at an English university. Tuition fees had been paid in advance by his family but in order to support himself he had needed to work and study at the same time. He had dropped out before the year was over. I felt that I was in the presence of a lost and alienated young man, in the presence of a very rigid, non-forgiving, God-like superego 'I never forgive if anyone lets me down' and that he had allocated himself his place 'at the bottom of the pile' as punishment for letting everyone down for not succeeding. At least this gave him a known place, that of a failure, bottom of the class, anything different meant moving to extreme vulnerability and exposure. We spent some time thinking about the experience of a 19

122

year old and what it might have felt like leaving home, carrying both family and his expectations abroad for higher education whilst inside that 19 year old had been a child in a state of terror and panic who had been unable to share his fears and uncertainty.

Tears that were shed here, but never as a child at home, were not for understanding but served as persecuting shameful reminders in this country of his failure. He maintained a lie to his family back home, by reassuring them that he remained the good pupil, enjoying himself studying and doing well. Yearly student visas proved provocative and empty passports carrying the hope that all would be all right and crippling him from acknowledging how things really were. He was convinced that his parents shared his views, in spite of considerable evidence to the contrary, and by his actions he prevented real parents coming alive, free to be themselves, to forgive and understand.

Somewhat to my surprise Tariq came to all four meetings. On reflection I thought he was relieved that I had been free enough to challenge his fixed views, to think about his anger and look at the cruelty he meted out, not only to himself, but to his family back home. I could be allowed some position of helpfulness as a foreigner unfamiliar with class and cultural differences in his country of origin so that I had no predetermined place to allocate him. In the fourth meeting there was a noticeable shift from his demand for me to make things right by telling him what to do to the idea that it might be possible for change to take place little by little rather than being either all or nothing. In Tariq's words 'talking to someone lets in fresh air and another point of view'. In this last meeting we thought about ongoing help and I suggested an agency which is particularly concerned with work around cultural issues where, with a therapist who could speak his mother tongue, he might find a place for the child to be heard and understood.

The fourth and last meeting faces both client and counsellor with the limitations of the service and with what can and cannot be done in the time available. In brief work the counsellor must always keep in mind an ending from the beginning of the contract and work within this to observe and clarify the client's situation. Like Sharon with her ugliness Tariq wrote himself off as a failure although he too was open to thought and wanted understanding. However both made it clear in the fourth meeting that, in their previous experience, help had not been forthcoming and Tariq in particular showed me how good he was at cutting off from any support system or safety net for himself, casting himself out and making himself yet again a refugee. How could you take such a little when you needed so much? Saying goodbye to work that has just begun

123

is not easy and there is always the risk that any understanding that has been achieved, often painfully, can be attacked and the links be broken. The counsellor too must manage her own feelings of needing to be needed and not wanting to let go. How could you give so little when so much was needed? Inevitably in this work the counsellor is left with much uncertainty but must be able to let go to leave the young person free to move on and to make their own decision about what they decide to take with them and what to discard.

Maria

Some clients have been aware for a long time that they are in need of help, indeed have known of the service but have stored the information away to be used some time in the future. Such was Maria who had kept a magazine cutting in her drawer for years. She is a young person who has almost managed the transition into adulthood but in so doing has had to identify herself with a demanding and idealising parent who sets impossible standards.

Maria was Spanish, the sixth child in a family of eleven and one of two children who went to university. The family was always short of money and she was very conscious of her parents' struggle to provide for all of them. Education had been very important and she knew that her mother had wanted to go to university herself. Her mother died of a heart attack when Maria was 20 and in her final year at university. She just managed to scrape through her finals by 'ignoring my feelings and getting on with living'. Restless and unable to settle in Spain, she travelled a bit and when she was 23 moved to this country. It took time to establish herself and there were a series of 'awful jobs' but she finally found employment which she liked and in which she felt appropriately challenged.

Maria came to the YPCS when she was 29 having already made a bridge into the adult world. Having found a niche there she felt grounded enough to return to painful earlier events in her childhood and adolescence and seek help. She knew that there were life decisions to be made. There were problems in her relationships with men, she was questioning whether she wanted a family and indeed, had she a right to come to the service, was she still a young person?

Maria was a tall, slim, dark-haired young woman with a pleasant manner whose neat dress conveyed an air of efficiency. To all four meetings she brought her umbrella and carried a large black briefcase, bulging with papers and which looked as if it could not close. For the

124

last nine years Maria had found herself on occasions, overtaken by bouts of anxiety which came from nowhere, took her over and made her feel totally alone. When the anxiety subsided she would think 'when was it going to happen again'. This anxiety was compounded by a terror that she might betray signs of it to other people and this was crippling her in her relationships and her confidence in work. The first meeting had a strange rather staccato effect when she touched on a feeling and then seemed to abruptly disconnect. Emotional life was compartmentalised so that 'isn't it better to shut feelings away' was a constant refrain. When I wondered about her mother's death, the way she described it crashing into her life, one moment a mother at the centre of the family's universe, the next moment tragically gone, she replied saying she knew there was a story demanding to be heard and that feelings were haunting her like ghosts.

The next week she was more lively, softer and more relaxed and although there was still the anxious child-like questioning she seemed to feel freer to move in her mind and work with me. She had felt sad and cried herself to sleep one night 'I don't cry' followed by 'I've heard it's good for you, it gives relief'. 'But if I start to cry I'm frightened I'll never stop.' She suffered from chest pains. She described an event which had happened when she was two. The memory was as if it had been yesterday. She was in the kitchen, her mother was upstairs very ill. She was sitting on the stool with her back against the wall and watching her father's face – there was no hope. There was 'this awful feeling inside me, it was just dreadful'. She said her mother had nearly died giving birth. In the fourth meeting she linked this memory to one of the 20-year-old returning home after her mother had died. Her father had been distraught and she had seen the same defeat on his face. She rushed to him and hugged him saying 'we'll have to manage without mum now'. Maria described a family held together by a martyr mother, hard on herself, hard working, a mother who never stopped. She saw her father as harsh and righteous. Both parents had high expectations of all the children. She had a special place in her mother's affection; that of mother's helper, doing what mother does, housework, caring for the younger children, doing well at school and even going to university because her mother wanted her to. When her mother died she threw herself into working – for her degree, for further qualifications, keeping busy, keeping going, so that by having something to do all the time she did not have to think.

In the third meeting I met that Maria, the Maria hard on herself who never stopped talking, working, needing to be the good one who could learn how to manage emotional life. I felt I had lost her, and that we were engaged on an empty task, perhaps one that Maria thought counsellors expect you to do but one which left no room to hear a child in a state of terror and left alone.

The fourth meeting was different, Maria was thinking and in touch with an untidy, messy self which she could not tolerate. She admitted – it felt like a confession – that she had a violent temper. She described her office where there was no room for her so that she was either in the middle of the communal office, unable to hear herself think, or in a cubby hole on the edge where she was isolated. We used this to think about ongoing help and her need of a space, free from her activity and chatter, where she could mourn and relinquish her identification with a sanctified mother so that her real relationship with her mother could come alive and free her to live her life.

Conclusion

Imran, Sharon, Tariq and Maria are four young people who have had dislocations and traumas in their lives which have had serious implications for their development. If left unattended these may well cripple them in the future. They are also young people who are extremely wary of formal agencies and to whom a service such as the YPCS with its ease of access, confidentiality, informality and limited setting appeals. Intervention in adolescence can be crucial. The presence of a counsellor, an outsider to family culture but of the parents' generation, provides an opportunity for a different point of view to be heard. This in its turn may free things just enough to carry development forward. As Tariq says 'talking to someone lets in fresh air and another point of view' which can lead to thoughtful debate and the possibility of change. While the service does not formally refer clients on to other agencies we do think with the young person about the possibility of further help and how it might be pursued. Many of the young people who come to the service do not seek further help but, having taken the time to stop, listen and think about themselves with another person, hopefully they have found something useful to take with them on their journey.

9

The Scapegoat

Margot Waddell

The image of the scapegoat can be drawn on to clarify a particular type of relationship which often characterises adolescent modes of functioning and relating. The way of relating is not by any means unique to adolescence but is especially evident in the teenage years. In the simplest terms the epithet 'scapegoat' is attached to one who is blamed or punished for the sins of others. This sounds like a straightforward enough description, but the group and individual, internal and external dynamics which underlie the phenomenon are more complex than they appear.

First I shall describe the phenomenology of scapegoating, both as an externally visible, inter-psychic process between people, and as an internal, or intra-psychic one between different parts of the self. I shall then consider what it represents in terms both of very polarised states of mind and of the dynamics underlying those states. The context for the discussion will be the Old Testament account of the Hebrew Day of Atonement ritual where the 'scapegoat' originated.

In short, the term as now used describes an active process: a disavowing or evacuating on the part of a group, or more accurately a gang (the difference defining the underlying destructive rather than constructive purpose), of unacceptable aspects of themselves; the locating of those aspects in another and the persecution of that other, who becomes the repository for feelings which cannot be acknowledged as part of the self. The mechanism is that of projective identification. It is also the mechanism which underlies all persecutory situations whether pertaining to class, gender, sexuality, race, religion, or political groupings. It is the source of the bind between the bullier and the bullied. Yet even though much bullying involves scapegoating, there are important distinctions to be made: this particular form of bullying involves a *group* blaming an individual or another group. It is a social phenomenon when external. When internal it involves a ganging up of parts of the personality against another part which is felt to disturb the psychic equilibrium. The processes are particularly visible in adolescence in that pressures towards conformity on the one hand, and individuation on the other, are often at their most complex and most absolute. Anxiety about identity arouses an acute intolerance of difference, either in the self or in the other: the seedbed of group identity if benign, or of gang, or mob mentality when the shared purpose becomes the need to be partners in crime. Such criminality of purpose often takes the form of cruelly bolstering the ego at another's expense. Teenagers, or indeed younger children or adults, will toe the party line, or succumb to the leader, under the sway of gang attitudes and behaviour which, as individuals, they would completely eschew. Just as in the Hebraic Day of Atonement story, one person is made to carry the unwanted, because guilty (unclean) and bad parts (iniquities, transgressions, sins) on behalf of others. The group feels persecuted by their collective wrong-doing, which is felt to set them apart from their own sense of goodness – from their object in psychoanalytic terms or, in Leviticus, from the Lord. In order to reconcile themselves with the 'Lord' the Israelites are exhorted to consign their persecuted, and persecuting, parts to a representative who will take them away and allow a sense of purity and right-mindedness to return.

The details of the original story are helpful in designating the state of mind in which this process happens, for the events replicate a characteristically adolescent mentality in which the projective mode tends to dominate over the introjective. The question, ultimately, is whether the infantile aspect of the psyche is driven to extrude bad experiences, or has the capacity to sustain them by taking in something which can ameliorate the pain internally. The nature and function of the twin goats, the scapegoat and the sacrificial goat, in the Day of Atonement rituals describe between them very different modes of mental functioning. It is with the scapegoat that we are primarily concerned but the whole story needs briefly to be told to lend distinctiveness and specificity to its significance. The Leviticus account both illuminates contrasting states of mind and highlights the importance of their juxtaposition.

The Biblical account describes how the Lord urges Moses to instruct Aaron on how the Children of Israel may be cleansed of their sins.

7   And he shall take two goats, and present them before the Lord at the door of the tabernacle of the congregation.

9. The Scapegoat

8 And Aaron shall cast lots upon the two goats; one lot for the Lord and the other lot for the scapegoat.
9 And Aaron shall bring the goat upon which the Lord's lot fell, and offer him for a sin offering.
10 But the goat, on which the lot fell to be the scapegoat, shall be presented alive before the Lord, to make an atonement with him, and to let him go for a scapegoat into the wilderness.

The verses that follow describe how the blood of the sin-offering goat is sprinkled on the mercy seat in the holy place, surrounded now by the cloud of incense which has been put on the fire before the Lord as testimony that 'he dieth not'. As to the other goat:

21 And Aaron shall lay both his hands upon the head of the live goat, and confess over him all the iniquities of the children of Israel, and all their transgressions in all their sins, putting them upon the head of the goat, and shall send him away by the hand of a fit man into the wilderness.
22 And the goat shall bear upon him all their iniquities unto a land not inhabited: and he shall let go the goat in the wilderness (Leviticus, Chapter 16).

Other versions have it that one goat was designated for the Lord and the other for Azazel (previously construed as 'Demon' or as a 'lofty, hard cliff', or, in an elided interpretation of the two offered in 'The Chummash', as 'a place that symbolises the forces of evil', since the goat is said to be pushed off a cliff; or, as a third possibility, 'dismissal').

The Day of Atonement marks the enshrinement of rituals for making amends, for making reparation for wrong-doing or injury. The Day was, as now on Yom Kippur, a festival of spiritual accounting. In Leviticus there is the exhortation that, 'you shall afflict yourselves'. These days there is 'affliction' through abstinence and, also of considerable symbolic importance, the chanting of a specially composed liturgy, the core of which includes *confessional* prayers, *thanksgiving* hymns and petitions to God to favour the coming year. But it is the *dual* aspect of the original ritual that must be stressed. For it describes two very different states of mind, closely akin to Klein's depressive and paranoid/schizoid positions. The nature of, and reasons for, the oscillations between the two characterise adolescent struggles and lie at the heart of the developmental process.

Some introductory examples of various aspects of scapegoating in different settings may lend substance to the more theoretical exploration that follows. A simple anecdote encapsulates the essence of the process: reminiscing, Mr Smith described being evacuated from Lon-

129

don during the War, along with a group of 7-year-old boys, to a household in a remote part of Yorkshire. As time wore on and the boys' unacknowledged unhappiness and homesickness increased, they started to become convinced that the landlady, or foster mother, was giving all their rations to her much-loved cat, which, in their view, she pampered excessively. One day the boys decided to kidnap the cat and drop it over the local viaduct. And so they did.

This simple and sad story suggests several possibilities. The boys' experience of loss and separation did not seem to be adequately thought about by the adults, themselves suffering from the trauma of war. In an attempt to relieve themselves of the unbearable pain of what was being inflicted upon them, the little gang turned their passive suffering into active cruelty. Perhaps they were trying to get rid of the emblem of their pain by despatching it completely out of reach, as if to kill off the inner gnawing, the hunger for food and love. Maybe some were punishing, by cruelly separating, in phantasy, the mothers from the younger siblings left behind – they were in danger but at least together, represented by the foster-mother and her cat; enacting, in other words, their murderous impulses. When asked by a bigger boy why they had done it, they believed their own answer: 'But it was eating all our rations!' In replying with such concrete certainty they demonstrated the way in which, under the sway of anxious states, an individual, or group will become unable to think rationally, reflectively or symbolically and resort to what are clung onto as 'the facts'.

The next two examples are drawn from William Golding's *The Lord of the Flies*. Again the story is set in the context of the Second World War. In this case the evacuation is by plane. The plane crashes on the shore of a uninhabited tropical island leaving the traumatised 6 to 12-year-old child passengers to fend for themselves. The setting is important for it represents the policy of physically removing children from the source of danger, as if that in itself would save them. Physically, for sure it did in most circumstances, but psychologically the picture was, and is, much more complicated, as the foregoing example makes clear, and as *The Lord of the Flies* bears out. For at the heart of the novel is the psychological realisation of the terrifying states of mind which, cut off from their parental base, the children have to endure, here so concretely and vividly portrayed in their island idyll-turned-nightmare.

A sense of menace is first felt by one of the 'little "uns"' – a shrimp of a boy, we are told, with a large birthmark on his cheek. For reasons of physical distinctiveness perhaps particularly in touch with persecu-

130

tory feelings, this little boy speaks in anguish of the snakes and of the 'beastie' that he has seen. In naming the unmentionable, he is touching on areas of terror and dread which the other boys cannot yet bear to acknowledge. Some unconscious collective process occurs whereby it is this little boy who dies in a fire which early on ravages the island. It is he, as the thinking character, Piggy, retrospectively realises, who has had to be killed. (The killing, unlike the horrific episodes later, happens by accident.) With that acknowledgement fear grips the others: staring at a swathe of burning creepers and in a state of quasi-hallucinatory terror, the boys cry 'snakes, snakes, look at the snakes'.

In the final crisis of psychic survival, the survival of the superiority of the thinking capacities over the savagery of the most primitive and impulse-driven absolute – preservation of the physical self – we witness, with the annihilation and fragmentation of Piggy, the murder of the civilised part of each child. With Piggy the conch too is shattered – the symbol of enlightened liberal democracy, and the representation of the combined capacity of parenthood, both beauty and authority. What is felt to have been internally a resource for the thinking capacities is burst asunder and is no more.

A fourth, and last, example describes an intra-psychic version of scapegoating enacted inter-psychically in the psychoanalytic setting. In the previous week I had had to change the time of a patient's session rather unexpectedly, offering him an alternative time on the same day which, as it turned out, he was unable to make. I expected him to object but not to be as completely stricken, desperate, sobbing and furious as he turned out to be. I was taken aback by the impact of his ferocity. 'I've been waiting for this', he said, through gritted teeth when he could finally speak – 'I knew it would come some time but I didn't think it would be so off-hand, so casually brutal.' During the session we spoke at length about his feelings of betrayal, of being not wanted, let down, thrown out, of how he had completely lost faith in me since I had become wholly unreliable, he had always known I was like that etc. Towards the end it emerged that he had heard me to say that it would be like this henceforth, although at the same time he *did* remember exactly what I had, in fact, said. He had simply elided the 'just for this week' with 'forever' and thought that, because, as he believed, I knew that he was unable to make the alternative time, I was effectively reducing his sessions without saying so.

The following day he came in, still furious: 'what are you going to be telling me this time ...?' Halfway through the session he said that he had invited his previous girlfriend, Margot (with whom he had broken

131

off relations shortly after beginning analysis with me) to come on a motorbike trip with him. He told me this very hesitantly and resistantly. He eventually said that he had not wanted to let me know about this trip because he thought that, with a sense of relief, I would feel able to hand him over to her. At the very end of the session he mentioned that he might not be able to come for a couple of weeks: he was going away for a skiing holiday over half-term and before then he had to stay late at college for a number of essential meetings. He was at first unable to see the connection between these statements and his opening offensive in which he had challenged *me* as the one who was deserting *him* without notice or discussion because, as he later divulged, I must have another more interesting or attractive patient whom I was putting into his time. He was leaving *this* troublesome Margot/me out of things and taking up with a nicer version of a Margot who would appreciate his beneficence (the holiday invitation) and ride around behind him, passively allowing him to steer and control rather than pushing him around in so untrustworthy and uncaring a way.

One can think of these few details in a number of ways. His leaving me may have been a kind of 'tit for tat' retaliation, but I rather think that he was needing me to carry the guilty, abandoning and hostile giving-no-notice feelings that he was not able to own himself (he had known about the skiing and the meetings for some weeks but had not mentioned them). Thus I became the baddy, the one to be punished or blamed. Now that I was invested with feelings that he was not able to acknowledge as being part of his experience of himself, he could set about viciously excoriating me for everything that he felt most internally answerable for.

The Lord's goat is ritually sacrificed in such a way that contact with the deity is preserved: the smoke of the incense covers the mercy seat, retaining a link with the representation of the living God. The state of mind described in the depressive position is one in which the individual is able to experience, indeed 'suffer', a number of painful emotions which are based in a sense of separateness from, yet concern about, the object or person of primary affection – in other words, it is felt possible to maintain a link with the object. The desire is to find some basis for an at-oneness with (at-one-ment) the object; to find some means for reconciliation through making amends. The sought-for reparation for wrong or injury involves, as an internal process, the recognition of damage done to the loved object, remorse for that damage and the capacity to retain a realistic relationship with it notwithstanding – one of ambivalence and struggle rather than the delusional extremes of idealisation and denigration or of denial and omnipotence. This is a state of mind, or attitude to life, which Klein believed would, in good circumstances, take precedence over the more primitive modes of the paranoid/schizoid state – a term which both describes the primary anxiety (as persecutory fear for the survival of the self) and the nature of the main defence against it (that of splitting). In this earlier state the individual finds various ways to evade the terrors which beset the fragile ego, involving a range of omnipotent fantasies: that it is possible to deny the pain altogether; to divide experience into such extremes of good and bad that the states of total bliss and of persecution are felt to be wholly distinct; to repudiate, evacuate, or expel the bad experience so that it is not sensed to be part of the self but rather to reside elsewhere, whether in another person or in another thing.

In infancy these are appropriate and necessary mechanisms for bearing the terrors of existence, but when they obtrude into later years they can be much more problematic to the development of the individual. If someone is unable to bear the fact that the object that is loved and felt to be the source of goodness is not only not perfect but is one and the same as that which is felt to enjoin pain and deprivation, then he or she will seek to evade such knowledge, drawing on the kinds of defence mechanism just described, the primary one being that of splitting (not just the object into good and bad, but the self too) and of projection. The phantasy is that it is possible to split off and evacuate unwanted parts of the self, simply to get rid of them, in order not to have to suffer their troublesome presence in the personality as a whole. Either no link is maintained with the good object and therefore there is no basis for remorse or suffering (for amends and reparation can only be made in relation to an object), or the bad feelings become invested in Azazel who/which, in the process, will have become a bad object, demon, or evil place, to be kept as separate as possible from the good. This could suggest, as some psychoanalytic views would support, that in the absence of any link there may remain parts of the personality which are simply not amenable to atonement, because of the bad and the good having to be kept so separate.

In fact, on close scrutiny, the different versions of the story describe different degrees of projection: the scapegoat-over-the-precipice represents the most extreme, psychotic degree perhaps – because wholly out of touch with an object – with the implication of psychic, if not actual, death. (Both murder and suicide come in here.) The Azazel/demon projection is towards an object who is felt already to be bad or who becomes bad as a consequence of the projection, thus entailing feelings

133

of reciprocal persecution. The scapegoat-into-the-wilderness represents the phantasy of being able to relegate aspects of the self to a mindless state, unattached to an object and yet theoretically capable of return (the return of the repressed).

Here we have the quintessence of splitting and projection, both in literal terms (one goat for the Lord, the other for the demon/devil), and also in more subtle ones. For the Leviticus story narrates not just a state of affairs in which there is a stark division between good and evil, but one which describes, or encapsulates, certain qualities which, in turn, contribute to, or constitute, those same divisions. The sacrificial goat has to do with maintaining a link with a live object ('that he die not'); to address shortcomings and wrong-doings, not only in deed (the sins, iniquities, transgressions) but also, by implication, in thought, in relation to inner states (the 'uncleanness'). The maintaining of this link sustains the sense of relationship – relationship between self and object – so that there can be a feeling of being answerable, and therefore a meaningful notion of amendment or reparation; an experience of grief for what may be felt to have been hurt or even lost; a desire both to repair and to be grateful for what has been, and what yet may be. (The elements comprise the contents of the liturgy already described.) Atonement, then, describes a particular kind of relationship – one to do with reconciliation between the sinner and the Lord, with a view to the restoration of good feelings through propitiation. It involves a notion of integration through the process of acknowledging wrong and seeking to make amends for the offence. This is represented by the Lord's goat.

The ritual of the scapegoat, by contrast, is constituted around a denial of linkage, around some kind of belief in the possibility of disavowing the bad or unintegratable aspects of the self by despatching them 'unto a land not inhabited', into some empty, wilderness part of the mind, where there is no figure present to judge or forgive, none to process or to understand. The wrong-doing now acquires very concrete terminology, designated as acts – 'sins', 'iniquities', 'transgressions' rather than as states of mind, – 'uncleanness'. The point of the scapegoat is that any meaningful engagement, in terms of guilt or responsibility, is obviated. The ritual represents a process of rupture with the good object; attractive because less painful. In terms of psychic reality the etymological uncertainty between 'wilderness', 'Azazel', dismissal' or 'precipice' ceases to matter. For being tied to the bad (demon) object could be regarded as constituting a banishment, or 'sending away' of all that is good, true and beautiful.

Rupture with the good object is precisely that which tends to characterise adolescents' preferred mode of being. Working things through with the present object (the Lord, parent, or focus of primary affection) is felt to be too anxiety-provoking, or perhaps too destructive, hopeless, or unproductive. Whatever the specific aversion, there is a common recourse to a phantasy of being able to rid the self of troublesome or disturbing feelings, and to relegate them elsewhere. The places to which they are sent, or 'dismissed', take on all sorts of shapes and forms, but they have in common a single desideratum, namely that they be out of contact with the self. For such is the essence of this kind of extreme projection: it constitutes a refusal, the denial of a link with an object that might require the self meaningfully to engage with those parts of itself which are felt to be unaccommodatable within any kind of comfortable self-perception. The shapes and forms will include a range of what might be designated 'typical' adolescent behaviour, similar in type and in goal, to the kinds of infantile states described by Klein, though different in manifestation. The underlying unconscious motive for the projecting is a defensive one: it represents an attempt to ward off overwhelming fears of disintegration and anxiety about survival, lest the good be felt to have been destroyed by the bad. The bad thus has to be split off from the good. If the wilderness is thought of in terms of a rough and desolate area where the individual wanders and loses his/her way, it provides an image for the out-of-touch-with-oneself state of mind which is both sought and feared by this age group.

In adolescence the most obvious wilderness is that of literally mindless states, found to be so compelling as a way of evading the pain of anxiety and confusion. The attraction to drugs, substance abuse, alcohol are but the physical concomitants to a wide range of addictive possibilities – be it computer games, television, slot machines, wall to wall sound, sport, Walkmans, raves, the net, gang mentality, stupidity, even cleverness. All these, and many more, may be used and drawn on in ways that are constructive and helpful to the growing personality, but they may also often be abused, looked to excessively and compulsively as different means of avoiding internal conflict or any imaginative engagement with the complex matter of growing up. The tragedy is that fear of the inner wilderness, of the sense of some unfathomable heart of darkness, propels the individual towards a version of outer wilderness which, in turn, threatens disintegration and from which it may become very hard to find the way back. (Joseph Conrad's *Heart of Darkness* offers a wonderful rendering of this predicament.)

A clearly shared characteristic of these states is that they function as a defence against contact or intimacy, whether with self or with other.

The point is *not* to be in touch with the object, for to be so involves all the discomfort of the depressive position already described. The splitting and projection characteristic of the paranoid/schizoid position may, by contrast, be felt to offer a temporary, if illusory, sense that those pains can be avoided. As with the scapegoat, the phantasy is that the pain of wrong-doing can be got rid of and sent elsewhere, unprocessed and unmodified by any personal suffering.

The Leviticus account suggests interesting resonances both with Conrad and with Klein's later work. Philip Stern points out an important aspect of the Biblical story: if the sacrifice of one goat was to atone for sins, why was another goat *also* needed to carry the sins off into the wilderness, or to be thrown over a rock or precipice. The implication is that it was felt that complete atonement could not be achieved by sacrifice alone. It seems that the sacrificial goat was not sufficient to remove the sins. The scapegoat was needed too. It was the Azazel ritual that ensured that the sins were definitively sent away. The import of Conrad's story is that the quest for the 'inner station' at the Heart of Darkness promotes madness if driven by intrusive greed, whether for ivory, or for mastery (of the interior of the mother's body and breasts), the kind of knowledge which is omnipotently separated from genuine links with the mother country/good object.

In a late paper 'On the Development of Mental Functioning' (1958), Klein identifies the destructive parts of the personality which she seems, at this point, to have felt were not modifiable even in a long analytic process. A split occurs between different parts of the self – it being possible for the individual to function reasonably adequately, in some respects, while exceedingly destructive aspects of the personality continue to exist in a different area of the mind – residing in the deep unconscious, and remaining unintegrated and unmodified by the normal process of growth. It may be that the Day of Atonement rituals encompass precisely this knowledge of human nature: that there are aspects of it which are feared as not being amenable to any process of propitiation or reparation, fit only to be extruded – thrown over some metaphorical precipice.

In just such a way one of Bion's psychotic patients believed that if he killed his parents he would remove the internal obstacles to a sexual relationship with the girl he desired. He committed the *deed* since he was unable to contain the murderous impulses by *thought*. Gripped by a very primitive projective impulse he hurled his parents over a cliff. This story represents the psychotic extreme of the projective process. There is a denial of psychic responsibility and an incapacity to feel remorse – precisely those capacities which lie at the heart of the atonement ritual. Remorse, literally the 'again-bite' of conscience (in its early sense of 'inward knowledge', inmost thought, mind, heart), is painful and seldom willingly undergone. Remorse represents a capacity to recognise the pain as justifiable, earned, necessary. The again-bite hurts.

The developmental experience of adolescence inevitably arouses feelings of ambivalence and guilt which are usually much more intense and conflictual than the experiences of the preceding, and relatively quiescent 'latency' years. The physical onset of puberty stirs not just powerful physical sensations of desire and aggression but, in relation to them, passionate fantasies and impulses, both intensely romantic and also destructive and perverse in nature. The beginning of the necessary separation from parents and family stirs dismissive and aggressive feelings which may provoke sadness, remorse and fear of loss or rejection. The struggle to find an identity involves 'try-out' identifications with a broad range of not-self figures, in an attempt to determine a sense of being which is independent of any role hitherto assigned within the family and also often distinctively different from the available models. Such not-self figures may be threatening to all, especially to the adolescent who, in an attempt to disembarrass him or herself of this onerous cargo, seeks to relegate the uncomfortable feelings. If we add to this the multifold ways in which engaging with the developmental task of adolescence involves experimentation across a broad range of states of mind and of behaviour, both licit and illicit, we can understand the impulse simply to get rid of the persecuting, biting guilt incurred. The propensity to do so will be far more insistent in those who, in the past, and particularly in infancy, have lacked the experience of an object who is felt reliably to possess the capacity to take in and understand, and therefore give meaning to, such polarised and split states of mind so that they can be integrated and thought about and thereby rendered more manageable.

If it is felt, for example, that, from the first, aggressive and destructive feelings can be, in some sense, accommodated in the personality, there will be less danger later that similar impulses will have to be invested in others, to be blamed and persecuted there rather than in the self. The link with an object, internal or external, which might have assisted the process of integration is denied, and instead a victim or scapegoat is found, the belief being that in blaming the other the self can be exculpated. The scapegoat is selected by a process not quite as arbitrary as the drawing of lots, as in Leviticus. For there is often only

137

a very slight differentiation between the sinner and the sinned against. It is more a matter of weighting than of substance. The so-called victim, the one who takes the blame, whilst being officially innocent, unconsciously seldom takes him/herself to be free of guilt.

The juxtaposition between the stories of the two goats draws attention to another important developmental characteristic. It marks the recognition of human frailty. A determining constituent of the depressive position is precisely that it is constituted so close to the paranoid-schizoid; so close that the depressive state almost requires the paranoid-schizoid, in the sense that depressive pain is rooted in this very capacity to know and to bear the evils of the human heart. Without the imminent possibility, under stress, of splitting and projection, the capacity to maintain a link with the object does not amount to the order of struggle which Klein describes as characterising the depressive position. It is the very closeness, or tension between the two states of mind which creates the meaning of the depressive achievement. For goodness is constituted in relation to evil, and remorse involves knowledge of that evil. It hurts to have to address the damage to, or feared loss of, the idealised object, which is mourned along with the loss of the idealised self. The pain, or difficulty of staying with the object is founded in the recognition of, and temptation towards, more primitive modes which lie so closely by. In the paranoid-schizoid position morality has a kind of attractive over-simplicity, it divides into absolute good and absolute bad. Whereas the depressive state of mind can be more realistic about, because aware of and yet not overwhelmed by, those simplistic categories. In bearing ambivalence it can encompass forgiveness. Many adolescents tend to stray into the extreme isolation of the wilderness place where there is a phantasy that it is possible to be absolved of guilt without really trying. And yet they find themselves stranded there without a good object, seeking substitutes in the demon/drug/alcohol/versions of Azazel or 'Lord of the Flies'.

What needs to be emphasised is the suggestion in the Leviticus story that it is precisely the knowledge of the scapegoat mentality which is necessary to the effectiveness of the sin-offering. It makes sense of Klein's situating these two states of mind as 'positions' rather than as 'stages', as they fluctuate throughout life. The various versions, it could be argued, represent different degrees of projection, from the psychotic extreme (over the cliff) to the more neurotic anxiety over feelings of guilt and deserved punishment (into the wilderness).

In adolescence, in particular, it often seems as though projections into the wilderness carry not just what are felt to be blameworthy deeds

138

(whether internally or externally perpetrated) but because of the confusional anxiety which holds sway, also carry good sides of the personality, which are then felt, both by self and others to have become irretrievably lost. By implication the Leviticus story encompasses this variant in terms of loss of contact with the good object. It is observable, particularly in groups of adolescents, that the individual who is extruded from the group – expelled from school, for example – may also be the one who has quite compellingly strong and good aspects of personality, be it talent, beauty, or intelligence.

A recent patient illustrates this. Fifteen-year-old Jane was expelled from her private boarding school for having become 'unmanageable'. She was a rather brilliant, strong-minded, vibrant and sensitive individual, who seemed very readily to have drawn some kind of group transference to herself. She was, however, also full of self-doubt, confused and liable to find herself frequently getting into trouble both on her own part and on behalf of others. It turned out that during her final 'gating' she had made sure that she infringed the rules not only by flouting authority by provocatively going into the forbidden territory of the local town, but also by sending a younger emissary to her house mistress to inform on her. Driven by the group, she was, literally, 'asking for it'.

With her expulsion the group disintegrated. They had not only lost the 'object' onto which they could heap their own 'sins and iniquities' while getting off scot-free themselves, but also a source of liveliness, imagination and intelligence, in the absence of which they individually fell into a morose, depressive and rather mindless state. Ashamed and humiliated, Jane was nonetheless now free from the mutually damaging bind between herself and the other girls. Supported by her parents she was able to reflect on what had been going on and, in her next school, found herself not only resisting the role of scapegoat in its classic sense, but also able to recognise some of her own more positive qualities. Against all the odds she began to flourish. She told me recently that, although she was very depressed a lot of the time, she felt that this was an improvement on allowing herself to be so hurt, blamed, and used 'without even minding, or noticing' what was happening. Being back in touch was difficult for her but preferable to being in what she now experienced as, and indeed called, a 'wilderness'. The good and bad aspects both of herself and of the group had, in a sense, been sent to the devil.

An interesting and not surprising characteristic of this case was that the expulsion left the remaining girls not only a prey to their own unacknowledged hostilities but with a weight of guilt about what they had done. By contrast, the crisis enabled Jane to find some help for herself, to get back in touch with her parents, to feel both regret and remorse for what had happened and to make a new start. She began experiencing the world as much more complex than the good-or-bad morality which had prevailed in her particularly restrictive school. She became actively engaged in the sorts of conflict-laden situations of choice, in terms of exams and decisions to opt in, rather than out, of studying, which confront the adolescent facing life to come, choices which had been so insistently fled from by way of the very mechanisms described in Leviticus.

The Day of Atonement rituals pertain to the social and religious well-being of the wider community and raise some important issues in terms of the nature of the external culture within which primitive aspects of the group may flourish, at the expense of the more moderate, thinking self. Throughout history the most vicious and bestial wars, massacres and persecutions have attested to the tendency for religious group identities to be rooted in the paranoid-schizoid mode of functioning.

Religious ritual and institutional practices, in particular, lend themselves to extremism, in that they so readily mobilise infantile tyranny and fanaticism. But other institutional settings are also adept at fostering a culture of bullying and scapegoating: government, armed services, schools, for example. In the absence of a wider or deeper sense of the social responsibility proper to the development of enlightened attitudes and behaviour, an atmosphere may arise which highlights both the bullying and the attempt to find a victim. ('Hit squads' are sent into 'failing schools' and blame becomes the 'cure').

This perspective raises two further points. The examples of experiences of evacuation, of boarding school, of a remote island and of a missed psychotherapy session emphasise the vulnerability engendered by distance from the potentially containing object. In the *Lord of the Flies* the boys who fare best psychologically are those who can keep their sense of parents, ('aunty' and 'home') in mind the clearest and for the longest. Once in mind, however, it is also the actual qualities of the containing object that are important, both as manifest, externally available and visible, and as functioning internally. For the thinking object which can genuinely help with destructiveness and guilt has to be one that does not lend itself to being experienced as reactive, persecuting, primitive, moralistic or over-demanding, but rather one who can genuinely hold uncomfortable mental states and encourage difference, forbearance, reparation, forgiveness. The central significance of such

140

qualities in the object is more emphasised in post-Kleinian thinking, notably by Bion, than by Klein herself, and the possibility of the containment of these unbearable bits of the self by the 'thinking breast' perhaps encourages a little more hope than does Klein's later vision of human nature.

The scapegoat describes a mechanism of disavowal and blame characteristic of a primitive mode of functioning which has much in common with typically adolescent states of mind. To locate the idea where it originated, in the Leviticus account of the Day of Atonement rituals, is to make the contrast between the scapegoat-associated mentality and an object-related orientation which properly contributes to the growth of the personality and to character strength. The original version of events in Leviticus is instructive in that it juxtaposes two very different states of mind in such a way that they are thrown into relief in terms of the nature of their relationship each to the other. The object-related state, the capacity to 'grow', is predicated on the taking account of, or engagement with, its alternative, characterised in Leviticus by different degrees of projection, ranging from the return of the repressed to psychosis itself. The process of scapegoating is sadistic and ugly yet, as Leviticus makes clear, it raises the question of the existence of, and the fate of, unassimilatable aspects of the personality, whether enacted in individual or group terms – those intransigent characteristics which spell the death or the life of the personality.

References

Stern, P. (1993) 'Azazel', in Metzger, B.M. and Coogan, M.D., eds, *The Oxford Companion to the Bible*. New York and Oxford: Oxford University Press.

10

The Heat of the Moment

Psychoanalytic Work with Families

Richard Graham

The presence of an adolescent in a family is a profoundly, although not uniquely, disturbing experience for all within the family. The developmental thrust of an adolescent creates a vortex into which all family members are drawn. Emotions are then experienced with such immediacy in the family that they are felt to be painful. For families in which an adolescent is in pain, or is causing pain, help may be sought from an agency outside of the family. Sometimes this help will be found within the extended family or within settings such as a school. Occasionally, the family will decide or be advised to seek help from a mental health clinic. It is there that the nature of the pain and suffering within the family can be thought about in the hope of finding a solution to the family's predicament. The aim of this chapter is to describe how a particular way of thinking and working with families has evolved in the Adolescent Department of the Tavistock Clinic. This model of working contains certain elements, which when combined can be used to help us understand and describe the difficulties occurring within a family. From this a therapeutic approach to such difficulties has evolved.

Given the ordinariness or ubiquity of the family unit within society it is somewhat surprising that those influenced by psychoanalytic theory have studied the family considerably less than they have studied individuals, or groups of unrelated individuals. In attempting to understand how families function we thus find ourselves in the position of trying to understand the family from the perspective of individual psychology at some moments and from the perspective of group psychology at other moments. Rather than attempting to decide which of these approaches is most useful I will instead suggest that it is necessary to keep in mind both individual and group psychologies when attempting to understand

143

a family; indeed, it is essential that they are both held in mind. Here I would suggest that a model from physics help us understand this situation better. Within physics it has been useful to consider light sometimes as made up of particles and at other times made up of waves. It is this ability to acknowledge the different characteristics of light concurrently that I wish to apply to families: a family at times will display the characteristics of a group and at other times seems to function more like an individual organism. In bearing this duality there is the possibility of a flexible approach that is unique and distinct from psychoanalytic work with either groups or individuals. In order to further understand the way of working it is necessary to outline psycho-analytic ideas that seem particularly applicable to families. Firstly, however, the work with families will be described.

The Work with Families

Work with adolescents has led to a particular way of working with families, although the model can be applied to other age groups success-fully. The model used is that of two therapists meeting with a family on a weekly basis, initially for an assessment period of (up to) four sessions. This latter structure not only offers the family a space for joint explo-ration, to see for themselves whether they wish to take part in longer-term therapeutic work, but it also provides a task which helps us to understand how any particular family functions as a group. When a family attends for weekly appointments, the intensity of the relation-ship towards the therapists deepens, and this facilitates the exploration of the beliefs and phantasies that so dominate the family life. Comments from the therapists tend to be directed to those areas where there is most feeling, and this often involves comments about interactions within the family, or the interactions towards or between the therapists. There is less emphasis on exploring the family's history (or the gener-ating of hypotheses about the origins of a difficulty) unless it is emo-tionally immediate enough for the family to use the suggestions without turning them into a comfortable story that they can repeat to themselves in order to reduce the prospect of discovering more disturbing truths. To illustrate this further, I will now describe some work which illumi-nates many of these points.

The A Family were referred to a clinic just outside of London by their GP, at the request of father; he wanted help with the 'highly disturbed psychodynamics' within the family. The family consisted of Father, a middle-aged successful pharmacist, Mother, from a professional family in South America, and their two sons Robert (18) and Simon (16). Their story unfolds with the first session.

> The two therapists (one male, one female) collected the family from the waiting room. Father started to speak as soon as everyone was seated, talking about Robert's behavioural problems, which had gone on for years, and were causing much unhappiness within the family, mostly between Robert and Maria. Father added, 'This might only be my view, because everyone will have different perceptions'. He then spoke further of how he and his wife had different views as to how to address the problem of Robert, and that this was a specific point of conflict between them. The problem seemed to have been there forever and it was something that had never been sorted out. The young man who the therapists took to be Robert was nodding during Father's account, yet still no introductions were made. Mrs A then spoke passionately of how her husband never backs her up, of how she cannot stand this sort of thing (bad behaviour), particularly when it is displayed on the streets, and she speaks further of how she will fight to stop this sort of thing. Eventually the male therapist manages to say that he is not clear who is who, especially as the parents are possibly referred to by their first names some of the time, and father apologises and makes some introductions. The female therapist is struck by the foreverness of the feeling around Robert's problem.

This account of the first few moments of contact with a family beautifully illustrates the speed at which interactions occur within a family, and with the therapists; the family behave as if the therapists know everyone, or perhaps are even part of the family. When the boundary between the two groups (the family group and the therapists group) is highlighted by the male therapist asking who everyone is, father takes it as a criticism and apologises. There is already then the suggestion of something persecuting in the family, of boundaries being loose or non-existent; the problem had no beginning or end, no definition. To understand these processes further, we must consider the two models which underpin the work.

Contributions from Group Relations Theory

Ideas that have emerged from the study of groups, and the relationship between groups, contribute powerfully to our understanding of the family. Freud added considerably to our understanding of groups, but more recently it is perhaps the figure of Wilfred Bion who has provided us with many of the most useful ideas for the understanding of dynamics in groups, and individuals (Bion, 1961). The ideas developed by Bion

145

stem from his work as an army psychiatrist, during World War II, during which time he, with others, helped to develop procedures for the selection of officers who could lead troops. This work on the nature of leadership and the relationship of this to groups has proved to be both groundbreaking and a spur to later developments in the field. It is Bion's ability to understand the position of the individual within a group (by which he meant any gathering of more than a few people), and the relationship of the group towards the individual allows us to understand the core, yet exquisitely painful dilemma of family life. This aspect of emotional life, is best described as a tension between the simultaneous desires for both individual expression and a longing for total immersion within the activities of the group; here, the family. Neither desire can be satisfied if the other is acknowledged, and the successful functioning of any group may depend upon how much the group gives scope for the expression of individual need. The family thus needs to maintain a space for both the individual needs of its members, whilst also maintaining some sense of a secure group identity. This experience of a family identity, of the family as a group, is important. Sometimes a family comes for help, almost with a sense of despair that they are a family in name alone, wanting someone to tell them that they *are* a family. At the other end of the spectrum, when a child, and especially an adolescent is wanting to express some individuality, a rigid or overbearing emphasis of the family as a group ('we do everything as a family') makes it impossible for the adolescent to take up a necessary and more individual position, and the family seek help. Anna Dartington has described this important part of adolescent development as that in which the adolescent takes up the position of the 'Outsider' (Dartington, 1994); a forthright statement of individuality pushes the adolescent towards the edge of the family group. Bion felt that it was helpful for the individual to grasp the nature of this dilemma, of wanting to be an individual, or separate, yet still feeling congruent with the group, of whatever type.

The fear and discomfort in a family, related to an adolescent's wish to be different, separate, or individual can be balanced by the experience of relief when someone can name the problem. Yet this very striving for individuality shatters the sense of a coherent group identity in the family, as very movingly described in The Beatles song 'She's Leaving Home'. Bion further added to our understanding by revealing how much of a groups life is spent in rather mindless states in which magical ideas and fantasies take over from rational thought, work or learning from experience. Such ideas or *basic assumptions* hold a great

146

power over groups, and they are not easily dispelled even when they seem to go against the experience of reality, and even lay dormant when more obviously rational activity is in place. Basic assumptions are shared by all members of a group, quite unconsciously, exerting their power in a covert manner to all those in the group. Families may function similarly, holding its members in the thrall of unspoken values, ambitions and fears.

Wilfred Bion's work led to further explorations of unconscious dynamics in groups, particularly through the development of *group relations conferences* by the Tavistock Institute of Human Relations and the Tavistock Clinic. During these the members and the staff of the conference examine the experiences that occur within groups and between groups. This latter study of *inter-group processes* (the relationships between separate groups or organisations), notably in the work of Rice and Miller, has given us further ideas with which we can further understand a family's difficulties. This is especially so when attempting to understand how a family attending a clinic, or using any other community resource such as a school, experiences the other organisation. The perspective is one of acknowledging that the family is one organisation negotiating with another organisation. The nature of these negotiations reveals how the family perceives itself, and of how it perceives the other organisation. Unless these perceptions are made explicit, there is a danger that all information, even that thought to be helpful, is seen in this light.

> In their third family session only two members of the Z family attended; father and daughter. The parents were separated and Mother had a history of Mental Illness. The daughter Susan started to complain bitterly, with a palpable sob in her voice that her father didn't love her enough. Whilst this seemed unusually intense for a fifteen year old, the therapists felt increasingly under pressure to condemn the father who was manifestly 'in the dock'. The therapists both commented on how the session had been converted into a courtroom, in which both family members appealed to the therapists as judges. Any comment from the therapists was seen as judgement, and not a means to further understanding. Despite this intervention both father and daughter continued to behave in rather barrister-like ways, presenting evidence, experiencing the therapists' remarks as cross-examination.

Contributions from group relations theory illuminate the struggles of an adolescent, who feels an urge to become more separate from the family group, when the family relates to all outside organisations (perhaps the outside world as a whole) as hostile, and that only certain

147

behaviours are tolerated within the family – 'this is how *we* do things'. The less certain a family experiences itself as an organisation, the more vague are the differentiations of role and task within the family, particularly those related to the expression of parental authority. The vagueness then infiltrates communication, both inside the family, and with others outside of it, and this becomes problematic. Part of the problem may be that the family is still trying to uphold ideas and beliefs (perhaps not dissimilar to basic assumptions) which are no longer tenable. A.K. Rice (1969) wrote of how many industrial organisations were struggling with rapid technological and social change; this is more so for families, and especially so in the 1990s. He writes:

> One danger is that members of a group may so invest in their identity as a group that they will defend an obsolescent task-system, from which they derive membership.

One of the greatest struggles for all families is the management of change introduced by changes in society, and nowhere is this more clear than with immigrant populations. The tensions of remaining loyal to earlier values and yet needing to relate to those more current creates immense strain for an adolescent and their family, as feelings of loyalty and betrayal conflict with other needs. Sometimes this is most apparent when migration has been part of the parents' history, but other pressures, such as that in the family where academic success has been high, can be just as apparent. Frequently a family may not be in touch with the latent beliefs or task-systems (beliefs about what needs to be done in the family) that underpin their actions, and they experience bitter incomprehension at what happens; yet still they are unable to modify such powerful, unconscious beliefs. It is the painfulness of not following such ideas unquestioningly that is so often a part of adolescence. Yet it is also as true for the parents of the adolescent as it is for the adolescent, as the realisation dawns that the current family is very different from the parents' birth family. This brings many further realisations with it, notably awareness of how the family formed, how it saw itself as a family, and the disappointment of acknowledging the costs of taking any particular path of development. In light of this, it is little wonder that in many families, such thinking is evaded.

Group relations ideas have helped us to understand how such issues can be approached, and it is in the interaction between groups (and organisations) that a group's ideas about itself can be explored; for example, what sort of group it is, who is in charge, who can speak for who etc. It is important to explore these matters with a family coming to a clinic through asking how they view that organisation. The exploration of roles within the family, the ideas and origins of them, also provide the therapists with important information which can be fed back to the family. In thus introducing the family to themselves, the family, and adolescent may become more free to develop; to live rather than feel possessed by the past.

Contributions from Psychoanalysis

Psychoanalysis has immeasurably contributed to our understanding of individual experience, and ideas from psychoanalysis similarly enrich our understanding of the individual relationships in the family and the community. A multitude of ideas from psychoanalysis have passed into the public and academic domains, and I will not echo them here. Instead, I will draw on the ideas that seem most pertinent to work with families.

Any discussion of psychoanalysis inevitably involves the contributions of Freud, whose understanding of both individual and group psychology remains a core influence. In working with families one notices the impact of the Oedipus Complex, as described by Freud, upon the different family members, and it appears that the family organises itself around the *Oedipus situation*, as Melanie Klein was to later describe it (1945). The ripples of the Oedipus situation are seen in every individual throughout life, and so one sees the struggles in the parents as much in the children, and most certainly in adolescents. Whilst the caricatured core of the Oedipus Complex (wanting intimacy with the opposite sex parent, whilst feeling murderous rivalry toward the same sex parent) still holds true, Britton (1989) and others have recently increased our understanding of the subtleties and pains inherent in the acknowledgement of the Oedipus situation.

Perhaps the most important aspect of the Oedipus situation is the struggle to acknowledge, partially or totally, the sexual relationship between the parents, which so easily leaves the small child feeling jealous, envious, inadequate, and enraged. Part and parcel this acceptance is the acknowledgment of the differences between the generations, the differences between the sexes, and eventually the acceptance of the reality of death. These 'facts of life' are painful to all members of a family, either because such realities are pressing down on the mind of the child, or on the parents who remember their own struggles, and wish to evade the memory of them. The ordinary limita-

149

tions of the individual, who cannot do, be or know everything, have to be acknowledged for the individual to relinquish the grand schemes that promise an alternative to the pains of development. Work with families suggests that there is a shared phantasy or belief about the nature of the relationship between the parents, in the minds of every family member, significantly colouring the relationships within the family. For example, if the belief within the family happens to be that a couple relationship is an all encompassing, totally absorbing feast of pleasurable experience, it may be difficult for both the parents and children to tolerate the envy and painful exclusion that this phantasy entails. This may lead the parents to indulge the children, feeling it is cruel to impose upon them the ordinary frustrations of exclusion from the couple relationship. The consequence of this could be that the children become more unruly and eventually less able to tolerate any frustration. While it is a part of every child's development to have such envious phantasies of the parental relationship, it is the manner in which the parents view the pains of the situation that can make the difference to both the child's development and that of the whole family. As in the individual, thus it is in the family; the relationship to the Oedipal situation influences the entire organisation.

Melanie Klein's analysis of small children led her to develop further ideas following Freud's work on the Oedipus Complex. Klein drew particular attention to the difficulties of bearing loss, and in a family such losses may come with weaning, but perhaps most painfully for any child is the birth of another child (Klein, 1959). Meltzer and Harris have written of how different families manage such anxieties and feelings and have suggested that families could be categorised in their abilities to bear or evade the pains of loss, amongst others, and of how they organise themselves in order to do this (Meltzer and Harris, 1986).

Projective Identification

To understand this further, the later work of Klein is crucial. When Klein introduced the concept of projective identification in 1946, she introduced a tool with which many previously incomprehensible psychological processes could be understood (Klein, 1946). Essentially, projective identification describes a process by which an individual, unconsciously attributes to another a feeling, thought or phantasy whilst disowning its existence in themselves because it is intolerable to the self. While Klein described this as an intrapsychic process, occurring in phantasy alone, it is now believed to be often accompanied by behaviours which effectively drive the message home, and force the recipient to enact the projection in some manner. Reasonable or unusually calm behaviour during an argument ensures that any anger projected into the other person stays there, partly because this position is so provocative. Many and subtle are the dynamics of projective identification, and here I wish to focus on a number of aspects.

Firstly, the concept gives us a tool to explore how roles are taken up in families, and why a particular child feels compelled to be the clown, cheering everyone up, for example, or another member is quietly despairing, loaded with a sense of responsibility for all that happens. Clearly individual temperament enters into this, and specific temperaments make themselves available for certain rather than other projections or attributions. To carry a specific function or feeling for all of the family clearly influences development and hampers the emergence of other aspects of the personality.

Secondly, as Steiner (1996) has written, the degree to which projections are kept in their place over periods of time has enormous implications for the possibilities for change. A family that states a certain member 'has always been like this', and behave to ensure that they continue to be so distorts the development of all. Ordinary individuation and separation from the family at adolescence is then impossible, unless achieved violently, because the family are too dependent upon each other. The adolescent then becomes institutionalised. Minuchin's concept of *enmeshment* very much describes this situation (Minuchin et al., 1978). If projections are more plastic, and are used on a more temporary basis, then they are more easily taken back and the reality of a situation acknowledged and worked with; a family member is seen for what they are instead of what they were needed to be. For many this involves a realisation that the family member is not what others wanted them to be; parents mourn the loss of an ideal child, an adolescent acknowledges meaningfully the limitations of their parents.

As stated earlier, Melanie Klein's work has proved extremely helpful in understanding the manner in which individuals are drawn together through the taking up of positions in relation to each other, using projective identification. However, this is only meaningful when there is the realisation that such processes occur as a means of controlling anxiety. Many psychoanalysts who have developed the ideas of Melanie Klein have shown how the personality or groups organise themselves defensively to control painful processes. However, it was Bion, who suggested further that such processes help to withstand the impact of change, and that change itself is inherently painful, invariably challenging the beliefs previously held. Joseph has significantly extended this idea, in her study of the processes of change to illuminate how all individuals have equilibrium, a sense of balance that they try to return to, even when knowing that such equilibrium is failing them (Joseph, 1992). Thus for every step forwards, there is a tendency to step back, to regress. Joseph however shows clearly that such forwards/backwards oscillations are fundamental to growth, and that there is no hope when stasis is achieved. Projections and other defensive processes nullify the impact of change, as change brings uncertainty, persecution and doubt; tolerance of these feelings is core to development, and the inability to tolerate them creates developmental arrest. Families exist in a state where at least one of its members is likely to be in a state of rapid change, such as early infancy or adolescence, where the biological engine pushes ahead powerfully. The ability to tolerate change is likely to help a family follow an individual through their own idiosyncratic development, and not impose a particular frame upon it. However, all families will feel the pull to maintain the status quo, and this is likely to be part of any encounter with an outside agency such as a clinic, where the therapists will be subtly pushed into taking up a position that helps the family maintain its status quo.

Transference

Freud's discovery of the *transference* – the process by which feelings and expectations in relation to a figure in the mind are transferred onto the analyst – and later work in this field reveals how individuals see the world through the lens of their internal experiences (which includes memories of past experience and temperamental tendencies). The individual, no matter how hampered by this, will pressurise those around to fit in with this internal picture, and this can be detected by the therapist or analyst, through examining their own responses or *countertransferance*. It is difficult to be clear how these processes occur within groups, but they certainly do, and 'something' is transferred to the therapists when a family meets with them. This will be clarified in the following discussion. The influence of these ideas will become apparent in the following case history.

The B family were referred to a clinic after mother had discussed with her GP her son's 'inappropriate behaviour'. The GP indicated concerns about Tom (14) and his older sister Bel (19) and about the problematic relationships in the family in general.

10. The Heat of the Moment

In the first meeting, mother complained bitterly about Tom's behaviour. The therapists, somewhat startled by the vehemence of mother's position in the face of what appeared to be relatively ordinary adolescent behaviour, asked whether the family might also be coming for some other reason.

> Mother promptly looked very defensive and said 'Everything is fine between us as a couple', barely looking at her husband. Mother continued to talk to Tom, complaining 'You don't talk to me anymore'.

The therapists felt that this issue of 'the couple' proved to be a no-go-area, even though it seemed to be brought up quite spontaneously by mother. Instead, they noted that the family seemed to be pulled into endless arguments, while also feeling both paralysed and irritable as a therapist-couple, feeling that it was difficult to do any constructive work together – perhaps already echoing the relationship between the parents, or at least a phantasy about this relationship in the family. Despite the vitriol of the first family session something rather different happened at the start the of the second meeting:

> Mr B looked sad and said rather nostalgically that he wished they were the kind of family that did things together on a Saturday, and in a touching way how they had done so when the children were small. Everyone looked down and rather sad, but mother interrupted and spoke of how Tom had changed and that he was no fun anymore. Tom erupted, swearing, with his sister rallying to his aid. The therapists were eventually able to comment on the difficulties in the family of staying in touch with each other, and how they were easily pulled back into the accusatory arguments that so dominated the previous session. After a pause, mother started to cry, saying how much she missed her daughter at weekends, and how she felt that things were falling apart.

It became apparent to the therapists later that the distress of the parents was related to a phantasy that they had not become a couple through the ordinary means, but had somehow stolen this position. They felt false and empty as a result, and were clinging to their children. There was little sense that the parents could withstand loss, and their abilities to negotiate the Oedipal issues were still very frail. As a defence, the family felt the pull of a distracting argument, that clouded the tragedy that was felt to exist below the veneer of family life.

The Unique Qualities of the Family

While the study of the individual through psychoanalytic work and the study of groups, through studying experiences that occur in groups, undoubtedly illuminate many aspects of family life, the family is a unique structure, although often difficult to define. Parents bring with them a whole range of expectations, beliefs, most held only in the unconscious mind, to the family, from their own backgrounds. Any child will grow in the culture of such beliefs, which, underpin all of the actions of the family members. Many of the beliefs will be at the level of phantasies about the quality of certain relationships such as the mother-child relationship, or the relationship between the parents, and the view of the outside world. Such beliefs become assumptions, unspoken, yet very present in the emotional life of the family. The nature of these assumptions, and the relation of them to culture, is important as they are often suffused with a moral tone that demands obedience from the family members.

Just as Melanie Klein showed how each individual has a number of internal figures, internal objects, in their mind, the relationship to whom provides a lens through which the world is seen, so there is a similar process within families. At quite unspoken, unconscious levels there appear to be joint phantasies, or shared internal figures, which may represent shared beliefs about the nature of certain relationships; for example the nature of the mother-infant relationship. These phantasies define the emotional life of the family, as much as internal object relationships define the emotional life of the individual. What is more difficult to determine is how such shared phantasies develop, and what can influence them. It is likely that they are passed down through the generations in more or less unmodified forms, through the subtle interactions of family life, and in this way a grandparent may influence the development of a child who has been born after the grandparents death. Phantasies of children replacing earlier family figures, of being 'like' a certain figure are rife, and very much influence individual development. At certain extremes, these shared figures can take on more primitive dimensions, and the family might function as if under a curse, ordained from on high by the gods; as a house was cursed in a Greek tragedy, and every generation was doomed to carry the curse.

The question then becomes one of how one understands the nature of such shared phantasies, and how can one effect change when such powerful forces are operative. Joseph (1992) has emphasised the importance of establishing contact with individuals at the most emotionally

154

alive point, that is where there is most accessibility to contact with deeper feelings and that the understanding that emerges from such an approach is most likely to lead to change. The emotional honesty inherent in this approach is vital, as a family or individual may believe themselves to be behaving in a certain way, but something quite different happens in the relationship to the therapist, and this must be acknowledged. Insight into this, the transference to the therapist, without explanation, is a powerful engine of change. Work with families in this manner does provide a crucible in which the heat of both the relationships within the family and towards the therapists itself promotes development. This intense work goes on mostly in the relationships to the therapists, as representatives of an organisation/Clinic (intergroup process – as described on page 147) or as representing certain phantasied figures (transference) that can be explored. The therapists' emotional response to the family, and to each other is important information that further illuminates the nature of the shared phantasies that so determines family life. Comments from the therapists about the interactions in the room – between the family and the therapists, or between the therapists – introduce the family to a picture of themselves so far unseen. While this may be dreaded, without it there is little prospect for change.

The nature of the shared family objects, and of the processes of change and insight warrant more attention, and such attention is beyond the scope of this chapter. It is however important to acknowledge that change in a family at adolescence is inevitable, even though a family including the adolescent may pull therapists into positions where the status quo can be maintained.

The reason for this is that the biological changes occurring within the adolescent are such powerful engines of change that the emotional heat is turned up high within the family, and it is hard to truly resist this. Roles and functions previously distributed in certain ways become less fixed, as the child becomes an adult. Our view of change at such times is such that one does not expect a particular end-point to be reached, but that there is enough plasticity within the family relationships for adaptation or re-organisation to occur, in keeping with the realities of changing biological and emotional development. If such plasticity can evolve, then there is the hope that relationships in which development and change are a part, can flourish, and that the family can grow in whatever direction it wishes to. However, such change inevitably involves the painful relinquishment of previously held or cherished beliefs

155

and relationships. To illustrate this further we return to the A family, still in their first family session.

Robert is described of having had problems since the age of 13, and mother talks non-stop about her son as 'this child' and of how 'the father' does not provide discipline. There have been concerns that Robert will get involved in soft drugs, doesn't do his homework, and is never punctual. 'The father' apparently just gives Robert articles on drugs for Robert to make his own mind up. Robert is quick to defend himself against this tirade from mother, and says 'Oh come on, nothing has changed. I am not different in what I do, but I am older and I do have my own mind. You can forbid me, but it is up to me whether or not I listen; you just want to train me and make me like you'. Robert and his mother then continue their passionate exchange, and it is clear that both Robert and Simon refer to their parents by the first names, and further, slip into speaking Portuguese, and Robert calls Mother 'mamma'. Mother continues to talk of childrearing as an issue she will fight for, adding, 'You cannot defeat the enemy if your army is divided' referring to her husband's lack of support. She also spoke with dismay about letters from the School, and fears that Robert will fail his exams. Father is more supportive to mother now, and talks of how they do not know what Robert does, that he never brings friends home, and always wants to stay out late. Father feels they have been very generous to Robert, but Mother mutters in the background. Father then gives an example of Robert's time keeping; Robert does not leave until 9.24 a.m., whereas mother thinks he should leave at 9.16 a.m. – she is desperate to convey her panic about his possible lateness. Robert says, 'I wasn't late though'. The therapists comment upon how this time seems to be a sign or symbol for greater problems or risks, and mother agrees. The female therapist then asks cautiously, saying that she does not wish to sound trite, but has noticed mother's strong feelings on this matter, and wonders where they come from. Mother speaks of her husband not being a good father, and the other members of the family rather mockingly refer obliquely to mother's rural background. Mother says only that she had a good upbringing and appears quite lost. The male therapist addresses the critical feelings within the room, and that his colleague apologised for possibly sounding trite, and wondered if the family were worried about being judged. Mother then complains about how she has only come to support her husband, and asks why have they come? The therapists feel uncertain as to the nature of the problem and comment upon Robert's fairly ordinary adolescent behaviour; Robert does not see this as supportive, and looks contemptuously towards the therapists.

As this first session progresses, we can see the therapists struggling with the pressure on them to agree and fit in with the family, and one starts to see them function as rather a gang, for whom any authority is

156

intolerable. There is a sense of the family being in 'The Resistance', yet desperate for help from the therapists. When the male therapist comments on their sense of persecution, this does not lead to relief, but more complaints that there is no support. The therapists are thus increasingly experienced as a superior, excluding couple letting the family 'eat cake'. Robert's loyalty to this is shown in the last moments, when he feels he must stay loyal to the family, and sneer at the therapists. The phantasies of a sexual couple, with no real parental functions pervaded later meetings, and was seen in moments such as when the family joined the therapists names together to form a word that suggested that the therapists were always correct in their views.

As the assessment continued, it was possible for the family to loosen their intense and frightening hold upon each other, and to explore their background. While Mother and Father both felt distant from their own parents, and had spent much of late childhood and adolescence in boarding schools (where Father in particular developed near delinquent behaviours) other factors emerged. There was a strong sense in which the political manoeuvres by a dictator in Mother's homeland, which she could barely acknowledge that she missed, very much coloured her, and the family's relationship with authority. Wanting things to be right was a dictatorial assertion of power, and there was little sense of a benign authority. When the parents were seen on their own for some sessions, the battle between the oppressed (child) and tyrant (parent) infected the relationship between the therapists, and understanding of this allowed further differentiation and separation, such that at the close of the therapeutic work, father was able to talk of how much he missed being called 'Dad'. The family were thus able to re-establish in some ways more benign figures in their minds, who cared for the vulnerable parts in all; here care and concern exist, and loss can be acknowledged.

The loosening of certain types of 'family ties' allows an adolescent and their family to move away from the old strings that pull them in increasingly intolerable directions. Adaptation to the current society and to the internal realities of both family and individual poses quite a task to any family, and many may be in need of help. The approach and ideas described above offers a family the opportunity of meeting itself, and from there it is in the position of knowing what must be left behind as change beckons. The heat of our work loosens such ties and allows a new beginning.

Facing It Out

Acknowledgement

I would like to acknowledge the contributions of the following colleagues in the preparation of this chapter: Fiona Brodie, Jeannie Milligan, Eduardo Szaniecki, John Wright.

References

Bion, W.R. (1961) *Experiences in Groups*, London: Tavistock Publications; New York: Basic Books.

Britton, R.S. (1989) 'The Missing Link: Parental Sexuality in the Oedipus Complex', in *The Oedipus Complex Today*, London: Karnac.

Dartington, A. (1994) 'The Significance of the Outsider in Families and Other Social Groups', in *Crisis at Adolescence: Object Relations Therapy with the Family*, Box et al. (eds), London and New York: Jason Aronson.

Joseph, B. (1992) 'Psychic change: some perspectives', *International Journal of Psychoanalysis*, 73: 237.

Klein, M. (1945) 'The Oedipus Complex in Light of Early Anxieties', in *The Writings of Melanie Klein*, vol. 1, *Love, Guilt and Reparation*, London: Hogarth Press, pp. 370-419.

—— (1946) 'Notes on Some Schizoid Mechanisms', in *The Writings of Melanie Klein*, vol. 3, *Envy and Gratitude and Other Works*, London: Hogarth Press, pp. 1-24.

—— (1959) 'Our Adult World and its Roots in Infancy', in *The Writings of Melanie Klein*, vol. 3, *Envy and Gratitude and Other Works*, London: Hogarth Press, pp. 247-63.

Meltzer, D. and Harris, M. (1986) 'Family Patterns and Cultural Educability', in *Studies in Extended Metapsychology*, Clunie Press, pp. 154-74.

Minuchin, S.; Rosman, B.L. and Baker, L. (1978) *Psychosomatic Families: Anorexia Nervosa in Context*, Cambridge, Mass: Harvard University Press.

Rice, A.K. (1969) 'Individual, group and inter-group processes', *Human Relations*, 22: 565-84.

Steiner, J. (1996) 'The aim of psychoanalysis in theory and in practice', *International Journal of Psychoanalysis*, 77, 1073.

158

11

Play, Work and Identity

Taking Up One's Place in the Adult World

Paul Upson

Introduction

My aim in this chapter is to consider some of the internal and external factors 'at play' in shaping the attitude taken by every adolescent to the adult world of 'work'; and how this in turn plays an important part in the formation of their identity as an adult.

I think it would be fair to say that up until the nineteen sixties, the position an individual took in relation to the world of work formed a crucial part of their adult identity – their status and standing in the adult world. Now, however, we are in the so-called 'post-industrial' age, where a new technology has led to the 'information revolution' which is steadily and irrevocably changing the way in which people spend their working lives. As Erik Erikson put it as long ago as 1968 'In every technology, and in every historical period there are types of individuals who can combine the dominant techniques (i.e. the technology of the age) with their identity development and *become* what they *do*'. We have only to consider those young people who are 'at home' or 'in tune' with the keyboard and mouse of their personal computer, with the modems and remote controls, the mobile phones and fax machines – in fact anything which relies on the electronic microchip – to realise that they quickly become the 'silent majority' of their generation i.e. we do not hear from them because they are quickly absorbed, via the technology, into the adult world of work.

Identity Development

Although the ideology that accompanies the technology of the age provides perhaps the most obvious and readily available source of identity strength, we cannot ignore numerous other sources, in particular those which, as clinicians, we know come from deep within the adolescent, and are very much linked with the earliest and most primitive identifications that have taken place and now form a part of their character and personality. The intense internal pressures of the adolescent developmental process, and the external pressures which begin to be exerted by society combine in a way that leaves the adolescent feeling more or less obliged to 'make a career' out of something – using this term in its loosest and most general sense. Here again some of the concepts put forward by Erikson (1968) in trying to understand youth phenomena in the U.S.A. of the nineteen sixties prove very useful. He refers to a 'universal psychological need for a system of ideas that provides a convincing world image' – in simple terms 'This is how the world makes sense to me'. He emphasises that 'without an ideological simplification of the universe, the adolescent ego cannot organise experience according to its specific capacities and its expanding involvement'.

It is not only the immediate social environment of the adolescent, but sometimes also society as a whole, who via the media, tend to become aware of the preoccupations of adolescents when there is clear evidence of peer group activity, and what Erikson refers to as an 'ideological commitment'. The 'loner'/'outsider' on the periphery of adolescent group activity is less likely to be noticed or seen as significant. There is an increasing temptation to start applying labels, some of which may start out as purely descriptive but which, aided and abetted by media stereotyping, very quickly become value laden. Whether the identity conferred (however temporarily) is positive or negative depends very much on whether the adolescent is seen, in some way or other, as trying to find a place of their own within the prevailing economic order. To put it another way, is there any evidence that, however tentatively, awkwardly, misguidedly even, they might be preparing to ask themselves the question: 'What skill/strengths/capacities/abilities do I have that the grown-up world (of work) might be interested in? might want to know more about? might even be willing to pay me for?' Though even this puts it at a more rational, conscious, and coherent level of (economic) thinking than is evident in most cases.

The Psychosocial Viewpoint

In any event, these kinds of questions are bound to be further complicated by the fact that, along with the invention of adolescence as a

160

concept in the 20th century (Dartington, 1994) came the recognition that it was a crucial period for identity development. Sandwiched between the childhood world of 'play' and the adult world of 'work', and hence looking both backwards and forwards, it was inevitable that it would also be accepted as a period of transition when a young person might be trying on various temporary identities for size – not only to see how they fit, but also perhaps to hide behind them, and observe how the adult world reacts to what is going on (e.g. Sinason, 1985).

In relation to the economic order, the increasingly specialised (some might say fragmented) tasks demanded of the adult work force, not to mention the demands imposed by the new technology, put an ever increasing emphasis on the value of education. This is undoubtedly the major way in which the adolescent, with the approval of society, can 'play for time' or perhaps more accurately 'buy time' for themselves as they begin to consider the world of work. The notion of 'buying time' (with all its economic connotations) conveys also the essence of what Erikson was the first to call the 'psychosocial moratorium'. He defined it as 'a period of delay (either) granted to somebody who is not ready to meet an obligation; or forced on somebody who should give themselves time'. But he emphasised that it is not merely a delay of adult commitments; it is also a period that is characterised by 'a selective permissiveness on the part of society, and of provocative playfulness on the part of youth'.

As long as education is seen as part and parcel of 'buying into' the economic order (i.e. a preparation for the adult world of work) it would seem that society is prepared to tolerate a moratorium for its next generation of workers. From a developmental standpoint this is just as well, because there are many other issues to be faced, and tasks to be accomplished, before adolescents can truly be said to have taken their place as adults. Most crucial of all is the need for the individual adolescent to have the time and space to work 'on' – if not precisely work 'out' – the balance between the positive/creative/life enhancing and the negative/destructive/death dealing forces inside themselves. When Winnicott (1971) speaks so passionately and compellingly of 'immaturity' as 'an essential element of health at adolescence ... its most sacred element ... a precious part of the adolescent scene' he is in no doubt that there are no short cuts to this developmental process. As he puts it: 'There is only one cure for immaturity – the passage of time and the growth into maturity that time may bring. Triumph belongs to the attainment of maturity by growth process. It does *not* belong to the false maturity based on a facile impersonation of an adult. Terrible facts are locked up in this statement'.

Whatever the nature of the terrible facts, to my mind this statement rather ignores the enormous temptations and pressures that are faced by any adolescent who is gifted with a rare talent or special ability which can be seized upon and exploited for what the prevailing economic order might euphemistically call its 'growth potential' i.e. the capacity to make somebody a lot of money. Even without resorting to such cynicism, we only have to think of the successful young executive (the so-called 'yuppie' stereotype) whether from the worlds of finance, sales, marketing, advertising, public relations etc. to appreciate that, from a developmental standpoint, there are very real risks and dangers in putting 'image' before 'substance'. This applies even more so to those areas of the economy in which young people can very quickly 'make a name' for themselves, and then just as suddenly disappear altogether from sight e.g. popular music and culture, fashion, modelling, show business and of course, above all, the world of sport. Nowhere is Winnicott's warning better illustrated than in what can happen to those whose physical development and training of their bodies to perform highly specialised tasks is not matched by a similar level of mental development and training e.g. young women tennis players, young male footballers and others.

Clinical Practice

In our clinical work, we are often faced with young people who have either become stuck at some point along their developmental pathway or have been diverted or side-tracked away from it. They may be at a complete dead end – or else have lost their sense of direction altogether. Most of them are a long way from establishing any kind of secure identity in the adult world of work. I would now like to illustrate some of the points made above with a detailed clinical example.

S, a young man in his early twenties, was referred to the Department by his mother, who described him as having been depressed to varying degrees for some years. He had done very well academically at school 'without a great deal of effort', been offered a place at university to read science, but been unable to go back to college after Easter in his final year. His older brother's recent completion of a Ph.D. was said to be having 'a very depressing effect on an already depressed person'. S was described as having lost all motivation, as saying despairingly that he could not now, one year after leaving, face going back to *any* university.

11. Play, Work and Identity

On assessment, S described himself as having been depressed on and off since he was 14, and as having an 'irrational fear' of aeroplanes crashing over his head and migraine attacks; 'Things that are out of your control'. He didn't know why he had given up on university, he didn't understand it – he knew he wasn't as 'brilliant' as the others, but he could still have 'got a first'. Most striking of all was S's dismissive mocking manner, his intense scorn for other people and himself, as if nothing and no one was ever going to be allowed to *matter* in his life. The assessor was left feeling both hopeless and helpless at times (a not uncommon experience with adolescents) but managed to comment on how ruthlessly S set about annihilating hope and the possibility of change, and how anyone who dared to question this stance was treated with utter contempt.

It was evident that, so far from being in the process of working on the balance between positive and negative energies inside himself, S had already committed himself to a nihilistic approach to the world which, combined with his profound need to feel always in control of events, virtually squeezed the life out of everything. I often find myself using the phrase 'safe but dead' when thinking about patients with such a rigid defensive structure, particularly when what ego resources they do have are devoted almost exclusively to maintaining an intellectual defence of their position at every opportunity. From a diagnostic viewpoint, S could be described as firmly entrenched in a borderline personality structure (Steiner, 1979), forever trapped in an approach/avoidance conflict with his objects. It was clear that his hostility to any way of thinking other than his own would make life difficult for any therapist. Nonetheless, as is so often the case with older adolescents, if no attempt was made to redress the balance in favour of life and hope, the future for S would be bleak, and certainly a complete waste of his undoubted talents and abilities. He was therefore offered psychotherapy on a twice a week basis.

Initially S made some effort to disguise his ambivalence towards the therapeutic process by saying in effect 'I don't know if it will really help, but I'm prepared to give it a try'. He insisted that he did hope things could change, or at least that he could 'come to terms with his difficulties' and 'learn to live' with what he called his 'depression'. At the same time, he seemed quite determined that he would never ever put himself through what he regarded as the 'humiliating' experience of sitting an exam again, and it was quite clear that in many respects he saw coming to therapy as a similar kind of ordeal.

It therefore required the deployment of all his considerable intelligence and resources, and it was not long before he began to adopt a cold dismissive tone of intellectual superiority and arrogance, especially when he was trying to draw me into a quasi-philosophical argument about causation, and what he called our 'competing theories' or 'models of the mind'. His ideological simplification of the universe, indeed the stance towards the world with which he was totally identified, was that of the scientist who entertained hypotheses, and carried out experiments to obtain evidence which would or would not back them up, and in the final analysis, prove or disprove them. My psychodynamic approach was contemptuously dismissed as some kind of 'conspiracy theory' especially if I ever talked as if there could be some part of him working against himself without him being aware of it. To him this was not merely unscientific and therefore 'purely speculative', but 'totally irrational' and 'lacking in all credibility'. Indeed for S it was literally a non-sense, a way of thinking which did not make sense to him.

As a late adolescent bright enough to get to university, and with a scientist's ideological commitment (though without a degree) S was still in a position to get a reasonable job with good prospects. He had not as yet opted out altogether of thinking about himself in relation to the world of work, and indeed was quite worried about being unemployed, wondering how he would explain the gaps in any future curriculum vitae that he might need to submit. So he decided to get a job in a bank soon after starting therapy, though he made it clear he did not hold out any hope for banking as a long term career, and thought he would 'probably only be able to stick it for six months'. Since he was highly numerate, maths was his favourite subject, and he was into linear thinking with a vengeance, there is little doubt he could have done extremely well at a time when information technology was just beginning to revolutionise banking operations. But he was unable to mobilise his undoubted abilities in any positive way, very quickly got into his usual negative and self-destructive frame of mind, and was soon condemning his manager as an 'ignoramus', his colleagues as 'idiots' and what he called 'stone age banking' in general. It was clear he simply could not tolerate the constraints and controls on his established way of life and thinking that having a job entailed, and he fulfilled his own prophecy by leaving in disgust after six months. Though he did manage to 'put himself on the spot' by applying for several other jobs in local government during the course of therapy, he was turned down on interview, and this only contributed to his sense of humiliating failure and determination never again to put himself through such an experience.

The significance of his having chosen to go into banking 'for a while' became apparent when it emerged that he was extremely worried about the possibility that one of the major clearing banks would foreclose on a loan taken out by his stepfather using the house he lived in with his mother as collateral. The stepfather had apparently drunk and/or gambled away the money, and was now seriously ill in hospital, going senile, with a degenerative disease of the nervous system. S usually referred to him contemptuously as 'It' so he was not even allowed the status of a human being. In complete contrast he was able to express a genuine concern for his mother's state of health and 'what all this worrying' (about the family finances) would do to her now that she apparently was already suffering from heart trouble. In part this concern was based on a more paranoid identification with his mother as a 'victim of injustice', but it became evident that he and she had had a very close almost symbiotic relationship for a long time, so much so that the boundaries between them could quite often get blurred if not lost altogether. In particular, they tended to feed into each other's worries and anxieties about the future to the point where the atmosphere at home was one of total gloom and doom. S's father (supposedly an alcoholic) had left the family when he was five, and the total absence of any kind of father figure successfully holding down a job, combined with his primitive identification with his mother, clearly contributed to S's deep sense of failure as a man, and his almost overwhelming conviction that he would never be able to make it in the adult world of work.

His recourse was to plan, in meticulous detail how he would, 'if the worst came to the worst' make sure the bank would 'pay' for what they had done to his mother by blowing up their major building in the City. He clearly enjoyed seeing the worried look on my face when he talked at length in a totally serious and detached manner about the mathematical calculations he would have to make; adding, almost as an afterthought, that he would try and make sure it did not fall on St. Paul's cathedral. When I took up this reference to 'Paul' he looked at me as if I must be completely mad to make such a connection. S's attachment to death rather than life is perhaps best illustrated by the fact that he kept what he called a 'death list' of all those he considered had 'humiliated' him in the past, going right back to his schooldays. He made it clear that if he came to the conclusion that life was not worth living anymore, he would first work his way methodically through the list, the last name on it of course being his own.

S's basic inability to trust anyone or anything beyond what he saw as his own supremely rational thought processes left him feeling constantly 'frustrated' and 'irritated' whenever he had contact with something or someone he could not control in the real world. Most of the time, the idealisation of his intellect, and the resulting omnipotent state of mind enabled him to feel not only in control of all aspects of his life, but convinced that he could control any thoughts and feelings that I might have in the immediacy of a therapy session. Yet the fear of things getting out of hand and out of his control was never far away, and seemed to be equated in his mind with the idea of 'going mad'; so that anything I said which he had not been able to predict (and therefore control) beforehand had to be instantly and contemptuously dismissed as 'absurd', 'nonsensical' – and unfalsifiable. My countertransference experience was often one of not merely feeling bound and constrained, but of actually being tortured by him – dehumanised, reduced to a lifeless object, not allowed to have any thoughts or feelings of my own, but under his total domination and control.

For all the positive emphasis that S placed on the scientific paradigm, and for all his desperate yearning to see himself as the scientist 'par excellence', the negative stereotype of the 'mad scientist' 'at play' in the wild laboratory of his own mind seemed constantly on the verge of breaking through his rigid defensive system and out into the material of a session. For example, I learnt almost by chance, that his room in the attic was full of his most treasured possessions – bits and pieces of old radio sets. He would describe his obsession with trying to get them to work, the many fruitless hours spent combing old junk shops and street markets, getting up early to go to special auctions, compulsively trying to find the right piece of equipment at the right price. He was especially fascinated with old valves, and would describe almost lovingly how, if he got it right, they would 'glow with life'. The image of Frankenstein rising from the laboratory bench was never far from my mind on these occasions.

Sometimes S could accept the notion that he saw himself as someone rather 'special' and 'different'; but if I ever dared to go one stage further and suggest that in his omnipotence he saw himself as 'playing God' i.e. with ultimate power over life and death, I would be subjected to the full force of his scorn and contempt. What could I possibly mean by saying something so ridiculous? 'On the contrary' (and he would then proceed to take it out on himself) he knew he was 'just a speck of dust'; 'an infinitesimal tiny part of the universe', in the overall scheme of things 'of no significance whatsoever'. When he was full of self-loathing, he would describe himself in a savage and merciless tone of voice as 'peculiar', 'deformed', and 'spastic' – 'I was born a cripple, born with this defect'. Occasionally the scientist in him would try to re-assert itself, and he would say that whatever was wrong with him came down to a matter of biochemistry. After all, he was a machine just like everything else in the universe, albeit a very complicated and sophisticated machine built out of organic building blocks, 'a mass of carbon microchips', as he sometimes liked to put it. And I would then get muttered quotes from a spoof TV science fiction programme he liked, including his favourite: 'The one thing you cannot afford to have in a universe of this size is a sense of proportion'. No quotation I think could express more clearly S's terrible and fundamental confusion over where he belonged, his place in the overall scheme of things, the no-man's land he inhabited in terms of his sense of self and identity, the 'identity diffusion' or 'lack of integration' which Kernberg (1977) sees as crucial to the diagnosis of borderline personality organisation.

S was a very regular attender and remained in therapy for over four years, though on the face of it, the 'battle lines' between us became more clearly drawn with every session. My efforts to put him in touch with something more positive and hopeful inside himself were regularly treated with scorn, derision, and contempt. Correspondingly, this gave him the space to become more and more overtly entrenched in his nihilistic stance towards the world. Faced with such a constant barrage of attack and denigration, it is always a struggle for the therapist to remain alive and thinking – yet that of course remains the essence of the therapeutic task with this kind of patient. With S it was a question of not *allowing* him to win such a hollow and empty victory, which would have left him even more convinced of the omnipotence of his own thought processes and the uselessness of mine. Although he would have been the last person to acknowledge any changes in himself, S in fact gradually came out of his very despairing and hopeless states of mind.

The Formation of a Work Identity

The information revolution has led to a recognition, or at least a re-emphasis, by government of the crucial role of education in preparing young people for the adult world of work by familiarising them with the 'technology of the age'. But even if education is seen nowadays, and with an eye to the future, as part and parcel of 'buying into the prevailing economic order', as always young people still find their own means of 'buying' or 'playing for' time, of constructing their own version of a psychosocial moratorium. The term 'gap year' is perhaps as good an illustration as any of Erikson's dictum that each society and each culture institutionalises a certain moratorium for the majority of its young people. Whether or not young people do something acceptable, worthwhile, or even laudable, within it, is in the eyes of society, much more of an open question.

We have the psychoanalyst Wilfred Bion (1961) to thank for the fundamental concept of particular kinds of (unconscious) group mental life or activity which he termed 'basic assumptions', since the behaviour exhibited by groups seemed to be based on various assumptions about the world and their place in it (see also Chapter 10). It was Bion's view that society made extensive and sophisticated use of these powerful and unconscious group energies by creating institutions to express them in a more manageable and acceptable form – to 'contain' and we might even say, to 'civilise' them. He also spoke of an individual's 'valency' – their own unconscious need to express themselves in one or other of the 'basic assumption' group activities. From a clinical standpoint, what young people manage to create ('playfully') for themselves is every bit as important as what society *seems to be offering* or might seek to impose on them by way of its institutions. It is a worthwhile but salutary exercise to look carefully at each of the 'basic assumptions' outlined by Bion because they emphasise just how difficult it is to draw the line between what is supposedly acceptable 'for the time being' in a young person's behaviour and lifestyle; and what society – aided and abetted as always by whatever current stereotypes the media manage to conjure up – is always under the temptation to attack and condemn as unacceptable.

Basic Assumption/Dependency

Under this heading we have to consider not only the positive contribution that young people can make within the traditional public sector – health, education, social services etc. – but also the energies they bring to the many charitable/voluntary agencies and organisations which have sprung up to meet a vast array of more private and personal needs – from the disabled to the disadvantaged to the dispossessed. It is their idealism and enthusiasm channelled through such organisations which has managed to make up for many of the failings of what used to be called the 'welfare' state, and is now increasingly and disparagingly referred to as the 'nanny' state, and left to wither on the vine by successive governments.

On the negative side, we need only look at the interactions of young

168

people with the 'provisions' of the state which usually get into the public domain via the media. What determines whether the 'homeless' young person gets sympathetic treatment, or is attacked as a 'beggar' or 'dosser', stereotyped as a 'vagrant' or a 'tramp'? The 'Big Issue' issue (so to speak) has made it very clear that it is a question of whether or not, in some way or other, the young person is seen as trying to 'buy' into the prevailing economic order. How else can we explain why the 'young mother' who is one day perceived as seeking only the best environment in which to bring up her new baby, is the next denigrated as a 'welfare scrounge'?

Basic Assumption/Flight

Many young people in their 'gap' year do take 'time out' (no coincidence that this is the title of the most popular listings magazine) not only to travel and 'see the world', but to work for the many international agencies that are sponsoring numerous aid projects in the less developed countries. Perhaps, insofar as there is an 'enemy' here to flee from, it is the high technology industrialised countries of the developed world – in a word, capitalism. This 'enemy' is easier to see and identify when we think of the 'new-age traveller' retreating from the 'rat-race' into the countryside and a 'simpler' way of life. Yet it still remains difficult to work out quite who is the 'drop out' and who is the 'back-packer/adventurer' – unless we are aware that this apparent flight may be a natural excursion in the course of adolescent development which also expresses some of the protest at having eventually to find a place in the adult world of work with all its restrictive routines.

Basic Assumption/Fight

Here the 'enemy' tends to be defined by the organisation with which a young person associates themselves; in many cases they embrace a particular cause so actively that it would be quite accurate to speak of a total identification, however temporary it turns out to be. It can still prove remarkably difficult to decide who is a 'rights activist', and who is a 'wrong doer', who is an 'eco-warrior' and who an 'eco-terrorist'. Whether we are talking about those who not only protest but take action on behalf of animals or the latest road-building scheme; those who are deeply committed to protecting the environment on a global scale; or those 'fighting' for minority rights of every colour, shape, and form; it does not take much for public support and sympathy to turn to

169

suspicion, hatred and loathing – once society decides that a certain line has been crossed. Very often this is determined by economic considerations: the cost to the public purse of maintaining law and order, or to the construction firms in having and maintaining a security presence; how many jobs the new plant/factory/superstore would provide, and how much prosperity it would bring to the area; the importance to the economy overall in not falling behind in a new area of high technology, and so on.

Basic Assumption/Pairing

It does not come as a surprise to us that an enormous amount of the energies of the young are channelled into group activities and behaviour that fall within the category of creative pairing. Whatever fertile minds and playful imaginings give birth to, it is in the nature of things for adolescents to see their creation as 'brilliant', even if it is not an idea which will save the world and the rest of us are much more sceptical. We may be tempted from the outset to dismiss it as just another 'eight day wonder' which will not 'stand the test of time', and become 'a classic'. Whether it is in the fields of art and design, food and fashion, or popular music, these creative strivings and endeavours have an immediate and direct appeal to the senses. This is one of the reasons why the pace is always so 'fast and furious' lest the senses have time to become dulled; and also why the prevailing economic order is only too ready to go along with this shortened time scale to take maximum advantage of what is here today and maybe gone tomorrow.

Herein lie the dangers of exploitation of the young, though it must be recognised that, since commercial success brings *everybody* a lot of money, the kind of stereotyping that is usually applied to many areas of adolescent activity tends to be put to one side. If any kind of judgement is to be passed, it becomes more a question of: just who is exploiting who? For example, we are hardly surprised when the Spice Girls and Oasis seem to go along with whatever their marketing or PR men tell them to do or say in order to promote their latest records – that is what is expected nowadays in the world of 'popular' music. But when Nigel Kennedy and Vanessa Mae do the same in the name of 'classical' music, it becomes much more difficult to answer the question: Who is the exploiter, and who the exploited? A similar situation exists in the creative and performing arts e.g. Damian Hirst, Tracy Emin.

Conclusion

The identity taken on by a young person as they approach the world of work in their late teens or twenties has, and has always had, a crucial bearing on their identity as an adult in later years. However temporary or transient this identity may seem, society tends to view it positively if it is seen to be subscribing to the prevailing economic order. However, from a developmental perspective the dangers can be great if the young person is categorized negatively at this early stage because they are seen to be placing themselves outside the expectations and values of society.

In both cases the risk is that the young person becomes 'fixed', unable to continue moving on down their own necessary and unique developmental pathway. In a sense they become trapped by society, required to play out a role that has been assigned to them by the stereotype (positive or negative) that was originally chosen. The perhaps temporary identity of late adolescence can become reinforced so many times by the response of society that it is virtually impossible to develop beyond it, more particularly if it enables the young person to be a 'success' economically speaking. The identity then may become a kind of narcissistic 'short cut' solution, which is in fact *no* solution at all to the developmental issues they need to address. There is no steady long term process going on, no proper 'working through' of all the possible combinations/permutations of identificatory elements, and their gradual synthesis or crystallisation into an adult identity. Instead, there is the presentation of an 'image' or 'persona' which, precisely because it buys into the prevailing economic order, is judged to be a 'success' by society. From a strict financial/commercial viewpoint this may be true, but from a psychological and developmental viewpoint, it may not necessarily be the case at all.

It is worth adding that, by constantly re-inventing themselves in other guises, usually with the help of their latest pop video, some of these purveyors of 'false images' rather than 'true identities' can continue their successful careers into middle age. Madonna and David Bowie come to mind, whereas by contrast Marilyn Monroe and Elvis Presley remain forever fixed with the 'image' of themselves that brought success in their heyday. When the image on the screen, small or large, becomes all we have to go on, the only evidence we have about someone; when perhaps the technology of the age permits us to engage in electronic communication rather than genuine human interaction, will it matter any longer what is 'virtual' and what is 'reality'? I hope

171

this chapter goes some way towards pointing out the dangers of putting 'image' before 'substance', and premature economic success before psychological maturity in adolescent development.

References

Bion, W.R. (1961) *Experiences in Groups, and Other Papers*, London: Tavistock Publications.

Dartington, A. (1994) 'The Significance of the "Outsider" in Families and Other Social Groups', in Box S. et al. (eds), *Crisis at Adolescence: Object Relations Therapy with the Family*, London: Jason Aronson.

Erikson, E.H. (1968) *Identity: Youth and Crisis*, London: Faber and Faber.

Kernberg, O.F. (1977) 'The Structural Diagnosis of Borderline Personality Organisation', in Hartocollis P. (ed.), *Borderline Personality Disorders*, New York: International Universities Press.

Sinason, V. (1985) 'Face values: a preliminary look at one aspect of adolescent subculture', *Free Associations*, 2: 74-93.

Steiner, J. (1979) 'The border between the paranoid-schizoid and the depressive positions in the borderline patient', *British Journal of Medical Psychology*, 52: 385-91.

Winnicott, D.W. (1971) 'Contemporary Concepts of Adolescent Development and their Implications for Higher Education', in *Playing and Reality*, London: Tavistock Publications.

Index

Subjects

abandonment 62, 85, 87
adolescence 4, 30, 128: history of
   1-6; puberty 30, 31, 38, 54-5,
   74, 137, 155
adolescent: blame 42; concerns 10,
   54, 114-5; confrontation 54;
   confusion 20, 44, 54, 69; control
   60, 67, 119; curiosity 19, 32;
   development process 3, 137,
   160-2, 171; disappointment 15,
   54; disturbance 7, 53-5, 57-8,
   69, 72-4, 99-112; expectations
   26, 122; grandiosity 8, 13;
   mystification 20; panic 115;
   pseudo-cynicism 21; savagery 14;
   secretiveness 20, 75, 120;
   self-esteem 37, 43, 46, 48-9,
   119-22, 165; time-keeping 9, 55,
   93; trust 30, 31, 32, 56, 57, 62,
   120, 165; violence 59-60
adult/adolescent, interaction 4
aggression 15, 17, 44, 58, 60, 71,
   99-112, 137
alcohol 65, 79, 82, 138
alpha function 95
ambivalence 41, 44, 69, 77, 137,
   138, 163
anger 41, 44, 50-1, 67, 70, 72, 74,
   77, 117, 120, 123, 147-8, 151
anorexia 39, 79, 80, 82
anxiety(ies): 26, 28, 32, 40-2, 44,
   47, 54, 62, 66, 68, 71-4, 91, 109,
   115, 165; communication of 75;
   confusional 139; controlling
   151; coping with 3; persecutory
   80, 84, 133; primary 133;

projection of 81; survival 135
appeasement 62
assessment 4, 10, 25, 37, 40, 43, 44,
   79
attachment 80-1, 165
authority 14-15, 53, 121, 148, 157
automutilation 67

'basic assumptions' 146-7, 168-70
bed-wetting 8, 58
betrayal 17, 68, 131, 148
borderline personality 163, 167
boundaries 14, 17, 26, 60, 62-3, 84,
   112
breakdown 72-3, 82, 99-112
breast 61, 92, 136, 141
bulimia 80, 81-96
bullying 49, 51, 56, 65, 104, 107,
   127-8, 140

child 7: abandoned 120-1; given up
   for lost 81, 87; premature 33,
   58, 82; psychic space of 81;
   unwanted 12, 19
claustrophobia 69, 75, 99-112
claustrophobic 17, 59, 68, 106-7
clothing 21-2, 25, 43, 49
commitment 21
communication 20-2, 24-9, 43, 48,
   54, 58, 60-2, 73, 75, 86, 91, 105,
   114, 118, 148, 171
compulsive 91, 92
concrete 25, 27-8, 43, 74, 80, 82,
   85, 130
confusion 28, 41
containment 72-5, 81, 87, 95, 141

173

Index

Names

Alvarez 25, 35, 66

Bick 31, 94-5
Bion 62, 73, 81, 87, 93, 95, 136,
    141, 145, 146, 151, 168
Brent 65
Briggs 27, 32
Britton 32, 34, 149

Casement 25
Conrad 135, 136

Dartington 29, 161

Erikson 159, 160, 161, 168

Fancher 70
Fraiberg 81, 95
Freud 3, 15, 25, 69, 71, 149
Frosh 25

Garnett 19-20
Golding 130
Gould 66, 67
Grinberg 80

Halberstadt-Freud 16-7
Haris 150
Henry 94

Jong 14
Joseph 152, 154

Kafka 2
Kernberg 167

Klein 33, 71, 73, 106, 136, 138,
    141, 149, 150, 151, 154

Lawrence 84
Leviticus 128-41
Lorenzen 14

Main 80, 95
Mann 25
Meltzer 106, 150
Miller 2
Minuchin 151

Piacenti 65
Plath 76-7
Potamianou 80

Rey 88
Rice 148
Rosenbluth 63

Salinger 1
Segal 25
Shaffer 65, 66
Sinason 161
Steiner 24, 151, 163
Solomon 80, 95
Stern 136

Thomas 24

Williams 79
Winnicot 31, 161
Wittenberg 24

178